MEMORY PALACES
—— AND ——
MASONIC LODGES

"*Memory Palaces and Masonic Lodges* is a masterpiece of research on two topics: the art of memory and the lost Word of Freemasonry. Jameux's examination of Bruno's theories of the memory palace as a means to accessing celestial realms, coupled with how its application transforms Masonic trestle boards and temples into veritable talismans, is indispensable to understanding the history and practice of the transmission of knowledge in all its forms. This is a book I was planning on writing. Now I do not have to. Jameux has done the job for each of us—now all we need to do is apply it!"

MARK STAVISH, AUTHOR OF
EGREGORES AND *FREEMASONRY*

MEMORY PALACES
— AND —
MASONIC LODGES

Esoteric Secrets of the
Art of Memory

CHARLES B. JAMEUX

TRANSLATED BY JON E. GRAHAM

Inner Traditions
Rochester, Vermont

Inner Traditions
One Park Street
Rochester, Vermont 05767
www.InnerTraditions.com

Text stock is SFI certified

Cataloging-in-Publication Data for this title is available from the Library of Congress

ISBN 978-1-62055-788-4 (print)
ISBN 978-1-62055-789-1 (ebook)

Printed and bound in the United States by Lake Book Manufacturing, Inc. The text stock is SFI certified. The Sustainable Forestry Initiative® program promotes sustainable forest management.

10 9 8 7 6 5 4 3 2 1

Text design and layout by Virginia Scott Bowman
This book was typeset in Garamond Premier Pro with Noyh Geometric used as the display typeface

To send correspondence to the author of this book, mail a first-class letter to the author c/o Inner Traditions • Bear & Company, One Park Street, Rochester, VT 05767, and we will forward the communication, or email the author at **jameux .charles@wanadoo.fr**.

To Claude Gagne

Memories are lies, and stories are fit only for children.

Paul Valéry

Descartes required ten hours of sleep a night and lazed in bed until the sun was high in the sky. I regard this denigrated man as a visionary, of course, but it is not the Rosicrucian who will provide us with Method's final word. Between slumber and waking, the inner burden carries great weight and treats the sleeper's persona as a subordinate.

Philippe Audoin

Contents

The Influences Leading to the Art

By Francis Bardot

ANYONE UNDERTAKING HISTORICAL RESEARCH on the transmission of ideas is faced with a constant temptation, one that will always lead to mistakes if one surrenders to it. This is the constant temptation to give factual historical accuracy the upper hand over the subtle reality of the murmur of influences.

Or to restate this in the words of Antoine de Saint-Exupéry, "To be tempted is to be tempted, when the spirit is asleep, to surrender to the reasons of the mind."

There are countless examples of this. It starts with the legacy of the Greeks. In our desire to make them the ancestors of our rationalist thought, we easily gather together evidence of this aspect of their thought: the Stoics crafting language and grammar, the influences of Aristotle's philosophy all the way up to the time of medieval Scholasticism—there is no shortage of examples.

This overlooks the fact that Greek thought unfailingly maintained a permanent overlapping of *mythos* and *logos,* as shown by the sole true crucible of Greek civilization—tragedy. We are clearly the heirs of the

Romans, and the mishap was created when Cicero could find no better term in the Latin language to translate the concept of logos than the impoverished term of *ratio.*

In the same order of things, it is probably easy, because it has been factually recognized, to prove that the Ancient and Accepted Scottish Rite was born among the Masons that frequented the *modern* lodges. But who could deny that the reformist impulse for a return to a true speculative Masonry—that of seventeenth-century Scotland—is clearly the one that inspired the secession of the *Antients* and to some extent anticipated the Compromise of 1813, which engendered the Rite of Perfection?

Who, outside of Lubac and his readers, could recover the trail of the Calabrian monk Joachim of Fiori in the works of Voltaire and Hegel? Who, unless they followed Cicero to Rhodes, would have been able to rediscover the origins of the Stoic ideas Saint Augustine instilled into Christianity? What, other than reading, could confirm that Meister Eckhart's notion of God's birth in the soul came directly from Proclus?

Charles B. Jameux is one of those spirits whose historical quest in the Masonic domain—rigorous in its hunt for facts—is no less guided by a very sure initiatory habitus.

The study he made in the mid-nineties on the connection between the art of memory of antiquity and Masonic methodology shed a new, and surprisingly powerful, light on our considerations of the Royal Art (included in this U.S. edition as appendix B). The important work he had performed based on that of Frances Yates and David Stevenson inspired a wealth of new studies and publications, when they were not simply pillaged without due credit from the sources he made available.

The latest results of his research will be, in my opinion, just as fruitful for the Masonic reflection and understanding of those not satisfied with simply attending lodge meetings. It is based on two pillars: one is a study concerning the appearance of the Mason Word and its meaning within its proper spatiotemporal environment. The other draws its Masonic conclusions from an enlightening text by Claudie Balavoine, who is in charge of art history studies at the CNRS (Centre National de la Recherche Scientifique).

This final contribution retraces the emergence of a hieroglyphic script in the arts of memory during the sixteenth and seventeenth centuries, but its value to us consists especially in the description it provides of *the inescapable seizure, by the letter, of the domain of the image.* Like the soul of Plato falling into the body, the symbol was buried within the word. Here is where the mystery went astray!

The purpose of a preface is not to deflower the enthralling nature of an investigation, no more than it is to offer contemplation of it to someone unwilling to follow the path that leads to it.

Nevertheless . . .

We remain Masons because we refuse a world that is purely rational. So where would we find the inheritors of these images, that an art of memory nourished by Neoplatonism from antiquity made available to the Renaissance as a viaticum for a quest for meaning beyond forms and appearances? Where would we find those heirs who are first the guardians and then the transmitters in turn to those they deem worthy of them? Was it not our founders' plan to hide them by giving them the means to live clandestinely as symbols, in order to reserve their discovery to initiates?

In beginning this brief text, I spoke of the pneumatic line of descent of ideas. While the cathedral builders likely prefigured what we are, it was nevertheless in Renaissance Neoplatonism that the poetic and sacred cosmogony that forms the milieu in which our initiatory spirit moves were anchored.

In the debates of the Western evolution of thought, it is customary to show how scholastic thinkers, followed by the disciples of William of Ockham, who preferred Aristotle to Plato, decisively separated the world above from that of manifestation, which ensured it was no longer seen as one indivisible whole.

But it was Plato's victory over Neoplatonism, and Galileo's victory establishing the primacy of mathematics over experience for understanding reality, which was the true origin of Western science going astray.[1]

Charles B. Jameux's intuition allows us to perceive from this perspective a very enlightening and plausible hypothesis on the origins of the symbols of contemporary speculative Freemasonry. I wager that they will form, like his first study on the art of memory, a departure point for many works to come. This foreword is intended to help prevent those who create these future works from forgetting to give credit where it is due.

FRANCIS BARDOT is the president of the French National Choral Directors Association and a member of the Grand Lodge of the Alliance Maçonnique Française. A knight of the French Legion of Honor, he is also a 33rd-degree Mason of the Ancient and Accepted Scottish Rite.

---

1. Rey, *Itinéraire de l'égarement.*

FOREWORD

The Art of Memory

The Origin of the Masonic Method

By Patrice Corbin

FOR A NUMBER OF YEARS Charles B. Jameux has been exploring a specific domain quite dear to him—one that is the subject of this book—and that is the connection between the "art of memory" and the emergence of speculative Masonry during the seventeenth century.

His research sheds light on a specific aspect of the cultural history of Europe; more precisely, the history of ideas, which Michel Foucault says in *The Archaeology of Knowledge* occupies a fundamentally intermediary position to the extent this field of study is both the genealogy of ideas as well as the history of representations and philosophy. The inspiration for Charles B. Jameux's work comes from the English historian Frances Yates, whose studies focus on the history of ideas, and particularly on the Renaissance reception of Hermetic philosophy and its influence until the middle of the seventeenth century. Frances Yates published a number of books on this subject, including one specifically on the art of memory.

Let's briefly sum up what this means.

The art of memory was initially a mnemonic device used in

antiquity that consisted of memorizing places and images that allowed an orator, while giving a speech, to stroll through the sites he had thus memorized in his imagination in order to collect the images he had left there that would remind him sequentially of all the points he wished to touch upon in his talk.

Used as a tool of moral edification during the Middle Ages, the classical art of memory would be used by Hermetic thinkers during the Renaissance as a method to acquire knowledge through striving to ensure the reflection of the universe in their minds through the use of magical or talismanic images as mnemonic images.

There is an enthralling element of our cultural history in this study: how Hermeticism and religious philosophy permeated this entire unsettled period from Venice to Wittenberg, while traveling through the court of Elizabeth I and Shakespeare's plays, and how all this very likely led to Freemasonry.

Frances Yates writes decisively but reservedly about this mysterious but as yet unanswered question:

> No one has been able to explain how such "operative" guilds developed into "speculative" masonry, the symbolic use of architectural imagery in masonic ritual. . . .
>
> . . . to leave as an unsolved question the problem of the origin of "speculative" masonry, with its symbolic use of columns, arches, and other architectural features, and of geometrical symbolism, as the framework within which it presents a moral teaching and a mystical outlook directed towards the divine architect of the universe.
>
> I would think that the answer to this problem may be suggested by the history of the art of memory, . . . which used, not the real architecture of "operative" masonry, but the imaginary or "speculative" architecture of the art of memory as the vehicle of its teachings.[1]

---

1. Yates, *The Art of Memory,* 303–4.

In turn, Charles B. Jameux, building on Claudie Balavoine's remarkable work that sheds new light on the evolution of the art of memory, picks up the torch of the research on the intellectual sources of speculative Freemasonry with a theory that can be summed up in a single phrase: "the art of memory is the origin of the Masonic method."

This would mean that during the seventeenth century, in Scotland, then in England, highly cultured individuals shaped by Neoplatonism, individuals whose spiritual needs allowed them to move past the religious quarrels of the day, those described by Frances Yates as spiritual malcontents, presumably "salvaged" the initiatory institutional structure of operative Masons based on lodges, rituals, and the secret means of recognition known as the "Mason Word."

Because the art of memory was no mystery to operative Masons, this "grafting" would have gradually transformed these building "*imagines*" into Masonic symbols of the spiritual temple to be constructed, or moral values to be respected.

This search for the intellectual sources of speculative Masonry casts light on this pivotal time for the history of representations and philosophy in the West that took place in the seventeenth century.

This, in fact, was the moment when discourse and concept would prevail over image and symbol, and this mode of analogical, emotional, and polysemic thought would gradually vanish from the intellectual stage and find refuge among the mystics and poets, and in the lodges.

This was also the time when the status of imagination changed.

Giordano Bruno, and the English Hermeticists following in his footsteps in the seventeenth century, believed that the imagination could be a tool for reaching the divine realms and attaining godlike powers. At this same time the philosopher Malebranche was claiming that imagination was the madwoman of the house.

Lastly, by making the year 1637 (the year when René Descartes published his *Discourse on Method* as well as the year when the term *Mason Word* first appeared) a pivotal date, Charles B. Jameux casts light on a significant moment in the history of Western thought: the emergence of subjective philosophy.

Until Descartes, especially among the Hermetic thinkers of the Renaissance, man (described by Pico dela Mirandola and Renaissance humanism as the most marvelous thing in existence) possessed his own rightful value, albeit without making any claims that his was the highest value. Man and nature were as compatible as twins and were thought alike from the perspective of natural law. In short, the human was not confounded with the subject.

Descartes established a real, ontological separation between man and nature. On one side, we have the subject (*res cogitans*) who rebuilds all knowledge on the sole strength of the *ego cogito*—I only think because of the ability to judge that resides in my mind—and on the other, physical nature, the sprawling vastness (*res extensa*) devoid of all properties, an object of infinite knowledge without any moral investment—the eternal silence of these infinite spaces terrifies me!

It was then that the "twin" thought of man in the cosmos also found refuge in Masonic symbolism and lodges.

PATRICE CORBIN is a member of the Grand Lodge of France and the coauthor with Jean-François Pluviaud of *Les 101 mots de la Franc-maçonnerie* [The 101 Words of Freemasonry] (Paris: Dervy, 2017).

INTRODUCTION
The Night of Origins

THE NIGHT OF ORIGINS!

The night of origins? No Freemason,[1] in my view, has any legitimate right to exempt himself from considering this question. Why is that?

This question contains in seed form the very significance we attach to our specific way of doing things, because the Masonic Rite—especially the Ancient and Accepted Scottish Rite—is deeply rooted, in essence and by design since its very beginnings, in the highly initiatory value of the speculative use of the symbols and symbolism of building.

But this speculative use that was the consequence of employing the symbolic method obviously did not witness the birth of all its constituent elements at the same time, or in some sense, as one might say, all in one piece. All these elements appeared in gradual succession during a historical period that all (or almost all) agree took place in the British Isles between two pivotal dates: 1599 and 1730. And we will not even mention the debate between the (very old and problematic) theory of a direct line of descent from the professional guild masonry of the Middle Ages and the equally elusive notion that

---

1. A fortiori, as we shall see, if this Mason follows the Ancient and Accepted Scottish Rite (or Scottish Rite).

operative elements were collected for the purpose of grafting them to an initiatory practice that was primarily speculative.[2] However, it should be acknowledged that quite a large number of these elements exist. And although they were historically selected and displayed because of their innovative and primordial qualities, as well as for their specifically speculative dimension, the date of the appearance alone is not enough to explain the prolific corpus that today is called Masonic symbolism and modern Freemasonry.

In my opinion, they only serve as markers. They do not innately contain the way they were crafted or the "cultural" secret of their origins. In any case, they cannot give us authority to claim that our Freemasonry was born on this exact date and not on some other date. We only know that its formation began to take place around 1599 through a series of phenomena akin to sedimentation. It is also fundamentally accepted that we recognize Freemasonry in its practically definitive and finalized form of 1730. It was at this time that all these elements had become assembled into a codified corpus that made it possible to no longer detect in the whole of the body thus constructed the survival of any operative practice of craft[3] as such.

Thus under this term, which is certainly all-encompassing, but also practical and in continual use since "the night of origins," we should really not seek shelter behind the relative impotence of the historian, but rather draw a distinction between two different realities: on the one hand, the events, and on the other hand, how those events were perceived. And to be perfectly clear concerning our origins, it is therefore

---

2. This second point was introduced in the very famous text by Eric Ward, "The Birth of Free-Masonry," in *Ars Quatuor Coronatorum*, no. 91 (1978), which was followed by many others.

3. For example, Dr. Mackey, in his list of twenty-five landmarks adopted by many Grand Lodges in the United States, does not fail to mention this landmark that he places in the twenty-fourth position: "The foundation of a Speculative Science upon an Operative Art, and the symbolic use and explanation of the terms of that art." Mackey, *An Encyclopedia of Freemasonry*, 443.

suitable to distinguish the proven historical facts themselves[4] from their interpretation and contextualization.

There is a great risk, it is true, of lumping together the historical facts inventoried in this way with the myths and legends that accompany and mark the successive and often obscure birth of these facts. So we cannot be overly critical of the poet Paul Valéry for cruelly emphasizing the unreliability surrounding the "invention" of both social and spiritual human phenomena, modern Freemasonry being in this respect, and in connection with the known facts that have made their way down to us, poor in both real history and authentic memory, while at the same time rich with tales that preach an origin *from time immemorial.*[5]

> *Their [the Freemasons] real secret is no other but their origin.*
>
> THOMAS PAINE, *ON THE ORIGIN OF FREE-MASONRY*

This is precisely why I now want to revisit the text titled, "Les sources antiques de la transmission initiatique en franc-maçonnerie: L'art classique de la mémoire" (The Ancient Sources of the Initiatory Transmission of Freemasonry: The Classical Art of Memory), which I first published in 1995 and which is included in this current work as appendix B. This is a text that has not always been fully understood and remains a document that some commentators on Masonic historiography have therefore believed was not worthy of citing, despite its precedence.

---

4. This subject area is one that calls for paying tribute to the entirety of the research pursued by Alain Bernheim. His studies are placed precisely at the intersection of the conscientious and the scientific method, which puts him in the forefront of all historians of Freemasonry.

5. I'd like to make it clear that I am only targeting the ancient players of the history of Freemasonry from Anderson and Désaguliers to Preston and Hutchinson with this mischievous, albeit fraternal, criticism. [The italicized phrase in English in the original. –Trans.]

So just what was it about, in fact?

Because the question of historical origins cannot be totally—and scientifically—dated, I examined the question of *sources* in this study. Here, of course, hypotheses are permitted and only authorize their authors to tease out the spiritual influences (in the sense used by René Guénon) of a nature likely to support the alleged origins that were claimed, a posteriori, by the Masonic method itself.

But because my opening statement included an essential reminder of these sources whose existence had long been known—to wit, for the art of memory, through the books of Frances Yates; for its presence in the Scottish Lodges in 1599 as confirmed by the Second William Schaw Statutes, as shown in the more recent books by David Stevenson—I was at pains to avoid mixing the two conceptual fields, consisting of the likely sources on the one hand and the plausible hypothesis I had deduced from them on the other. I merely suggested that things could very well have been this way and that the quest for the truth does not travel through the deliberate intention to force the facts to fit the theories, but rather by the legitimate necessity of verifying the theories by putting them in contact with the facts.

My present wish therefore is to contextualize my hypothesis from 1995 by first of all reminding my readers of the acknowledged historical certainties on which that hypothesis was based. Next, I will simply seek to show how it potentially fits into the successive contributions of a protracted and fragmented birth process in a noncontradictory way.

CHAPTER ONE
The Temple of Images

*From Operative to
Speculative Freemasonry*

SO FOR WANT OF A "legendary genealogy"[1] at my disposal or the authority to positively state that John Boswell of Auchinleck, who on June 8, 1600, took part in the Lodge of Edinburgh at the Hollyrood House in the presence of William Schaw, was definitely initiated as a Freemason in the modern sense of an accepted "non-operative,"[2] I think it would be to our advantage, in the context of my 1995 hypothesis, to stick to the uncontested facts. Were I to deal more extensively with this point here, I could only subscribe to the presentation and formulation that David Stevenson gave in his book, *The Origins of Freemasonry: Scotland's Century, 1590 to 1710.*[3]

> The Medieval contribution, of craft organisation and legend, provided some of the ingredients essential to the formation of freemasonry, but the process of combining these with other

---

1. Lantoine, *La Franc-maçonnerie chez elle,* 4.
2. Gould, *Histoire abrégé de la franc-maçonnerie,* 204.
3. On pages 17 and 18 of the French edition, *Les origines de la franc-maçonnerie;* in Stevenson, *The Origins of Freemasonry,* 6.

ingredients did not take place until the years around 1600, and it took place in Scotland. Aspects of Renaissance thought were then spliced onto the Medieval legends, along with an institutional structure based on lodges and the rituals and the secret procedures for recognition known as the "Mason Word." It is in this late Renaissance Scottish phase, according to the main argument in this book, that modern freemasonry was created.

Now, while I subscribe to Mr. Stevenson's presentation of this process, I am still obliged to respond to the issue of the chronologically dated and referenced appearance of the fundamental ingredients he is discussing and that he regards as acceptable historical proofs (markers in some way) of the gradual emergence of Freemasonry between 1599 and 1730.

What do I think these major fundamental ingredients might be? What were the needs that each of them answered? Just what would then be the initial occurrences of a specifically speculative nature—or connotation?

In the second Schaw Statutes of 1599, specific mention is made of the use of the art of memory inside the Lodge of Kilwinning, in the form of a regulatory injunction applicable to the operative apprentices and journeymen of the craft. It seems reasonable to me to suggest that this art of memory was practiced in its classical Renaissance form as described by Frances Yates. It was known in the court of the Scottish king James VI by William Schaw, as well as by Alexander Dickson, who also frequented this court.[4] It thereby implicitly offers proof of the presence of the foundational and tutelary image of the *temple*—by means of a temple that is now imaginary and speculative rather than one that

---

4. It so happens that the Scotsman Alexander Dickson was the proponent of the thought of Giordano Bruno at Oxford and Cambridge from 1583 to 1585 and took it upon himself to become the defender of that adept of the Hermetic version of the art of memory in the midst of the controversies and polemics that surrounded Bruno's visit to England.

is architectural and material—as the womb of Masonic symbolism in gestation.[5]

What did the next stage of this gestation require in order to take place?

What was needed were individuals capable of practicing this speculative discipline, or, at the very least, a favorable and "enlightened" milieu that now consisted of non-operative Masons, into which the first solely speculative Freemasons would be very quickly induced to take the plunge.

This is precisely what happened at an uninterrupted clip in Scotland starting in 1634. These admissions, which are confirmed by the "archives of the operative lodges of Scotland, can be traced in accordance with the facts that illustrate the process used by the non-operatives to penetrate operative Masonry" (*Dictionnaire thématique illustré de la franc-maçonnerie*, 247). They show the emergence of a profile of the men summoned to become—at least some of them—modern Freemasons.[6]

But probably the most important event to take place in the first half of the seventeenth century (and still in Scotland) is the mention of the existence in 1637 (at the very latest) of the Mason Word in Adamson's poem "Muses Threnodie." At this time only its name was mentioned, not its nature or meaning. These would only be explained later in the same century that revealed the two words *Jachin* and *Boaz*, an Old Testament reference to the two pillars of Solomon's Temple in Jerusalem, which had been barely circulated[7] until that time.

---

5. "The three simple words 'art of memory' may be taken as proof that from the first, the Schaw lodges were at least dabbling in occult and mystical strands of late Renaissance thought." Stevenson, *The Origins,* 50.

6. With respect to the admission of Anthony Alexander and some close friends on July 3, 1634, André Kervella offers a reductive and most reserved interpretation: "[A. Alexander was up for consideration] as if on an inspection tour, no more no less; . . . The reception they were given was that of authorities anxious to verify the way in which administrative guidelines were followed in the field. In any case, this was no kind of initiation." "Protohistoire maçonnique: La loi du Métier."

7. In the earlier, and exclusively English, "Old Charges," the two pillars that are cited most often were in fact the antediluvian columns made of brick and stone that were said to be the works of the sons of Seth, or of Enoch, or of Noah.

What is the presence of these two pillars essentially telling us?

They are the appearance of the passwords and the secrecy that surrounds their usage. They are the evidence—something that would only be known later—of what was being carried out in this instance under the cover of the form of a transmission during a *ritual*. This ritual was certainly a rudimentary one, but one accessible to Freemasons alone, and it was during this time that signs and grips were exchanged. Finally, and here is where most likely resides the "fundamental ingredient" contained in the two pillars Jachin and Boaz—an indicator of the speculative significance attached to the Temple of Jerusalem and no longer a reference to the two antediluvian columns of the Old Charges—which clearly indicates, as I am personally convinced, the appearance of one of the very first symbols that was not a legacy from the customary tools of the operative craft. And as we shall see later, this symbol was of no little importance in the propping up of the hypothesis whose general outline I drew up in 1995.

We finally need to add to these assumptions that have been listed and dated above the indispensable condition for the development of this new form of Freemasonry, starting from these years (to be more precise, 1641, with the initiation into the Scottish Lodge of Edinburgh[8] of Sir Robert Moray, a native Scotsman, an esoteric philosopher and adept of traditional thought, who was traveling through northern Britain) when "gentlemen masons" (who were still then called Honorary, Theoretical, or Geomatic Masons; see Pierre Noël) were regularly accepted and received into the Scottish operative lodges. By the second half of the century they had formed "mixed" lodges that sometimes had a minority but sometimes a majority of non-operative members (see Stevenson primarily).

These fundamental developments of the craft in the Scottish countryside were of course consecrated and, we could even say, finalized in 1696 when a document, the Edinburgh Register House Manuscript,

---

8. For more on this point see David Stevenson, Louis Trébuchet, and Pierre Noël.

provides us a complete "catechism" in a single text (serving both as a means for Masons to recognize one another and as ritual instruction) and the "way to give the Mason Word."[9] We also know that by this date, and for several years preceding it, that lodges consisting of non-operative members already existed in Scotland.

So to sum up the basic postulates of the present text, this brief chronological reminder primarily offers evidence for three things.

The first is that the origin of speculative Freemasonry is in seventeenth-century Scotland and only in Scotland.[10]

The second is that this origin, founded on facts that were spread across almost a full century (1599–1696), substantiates (but only for Scotland[11]) the theory of a transition from the operative form to the speculative form.

The third is that a number of "fundamental ingredients" observed by Professor Stevenson are present in the gestating phenomenon:[12]

> The image of a mental temple as a support for reflection and a method for memorizing the initial objectives and the procedures for achieving the planned architecture;
>
> The reception of non-operative members into an assembly called a "mason's lodge;"
>
> Secrecy;

---

9. Langlet, *Les textes fondateurs de la franc-maçonnerie.*

10. Certain examples, which are cited less and less as proof today by historians, such as that of the events of the Company of Masons in London between 1619 and 1621, or that of the speculative initiation of Elias Ashmole in England in 1646, can no longer be validly retained because, on the one hand, they appear definitively isolated from other events of the same time, and, on the other hand, it is especially because they are difficult to interpret as belonging to the multifaceted context of a larger whole undergoing transformation.

11. With respect to the later case of England, I fully subscribe to the borrowing theory, which, in my opinion (since the article by Eric Ward), clearly explains the new phenomenon recorded after 1717.

12. This is something that the "political" approach of certain authors such as André Kervella, for example, have been slow to take into consideration.

The passwords and signs;

A reception ritual for the candidates summoned to be "entered" (admitted);

A written document serving as a memory aid (written in 1696 but testifying to procedures that appear to have been long known); setting the terminology of the symbols; mentioning an oath on a sacred book, the Bible; acting as a tiler; and mentioning the use of the "word."

That said, does this brief chronological overview of Masonic history then being made in Scotland allow us to infer we have exhausted the study of the *source* of the symbols and the way they were crafted, in the first row of which we should place the Masonic temple, which is to say, the site where the assemblies of Freemasons have their meetings?

Of course, the answer is no.

An excellent study by François Gruson published recently aims at describing the migration of Masonic activity from the haphazard sites where it was initially located to fixed locations consecrated to serve that purpose on a permanent basis, brick-and-mortar buildings meant to serve as the headquarters of "established" geographical lodges;[13] in other words, in accordance with the accepted terminology, in English, of "private lodges." I should like to cite a lengthy extract to illustrate this:

> We should in fact recall that Freemasonry is a nomadic art, at least it was so at the beginning. The first lodges met in London in the back rooms of taverns. In Paris they met at inns or in private homes.

---

13. In accordance with the hence classic English terminology, like that which the scholar Dan Doron of the Philalethes Society reminded us not so long ago when he evoked the times of the remote past when the British lodges did not yet have "permanent members" or "consecrated" temples in which they could meet on a regular basis.

At this time, the only specifically Masonic element of the lodge was the tracing board or chart, drawn in chalk then unfurled over the floor of the meeting place in the form of a carpet. In the earliest descriptions, these outlines were most often represented with the name "lodge plan," as if to clearly show it concerned architecture, albeit an architecture of the mind and not a simple pictorial device of an emblematic or allegorical nature.

These "tracing boards" refer to the archetype of the temple, symbolized by the Temple of Solomon in Jerusalem. These drawings were inspired by the numerous pictorial interpretations of biblical texts that were quite common during the Renaissance. This ideal, if not to say ideated, temple, which serves as a symbolic representation of virtue, not only forms the blueprint of a building or locale that is not yet a temple, but rather a kind of mental architecture, that is to say, one that has been drawn not with a material construction in mind but but rather an edification of the spirit. . . .

It was only during the second half of the eighteenth century that this idealized architecture was finally transferred into the decoration of the site where the lodge met, a locale henceforth intended for strictly Masonic use. The elements of the "tracing board," that is to say, the lodge carpet, materialized within what was henceforth to be called a temple. The floor becomes a mosaic pavement that is adorned by a rough and perfect ashlar[14] on the eastern end. The walls are hung with canvases or look out on to imaginary landscapes, as if to clearly remind [the Mason] that the temple is unfinished. The eastern wall is adorned with three lamps and, in conformance with the biblical text, the door of the temple is framed by the two pillars of Jachin and Boaz. Lastly, the cornice is given the knotted rope that surrounds the carpet of the lodge. . . .

This is how, with the spatialization and materialization of an initially mental device, the place of Masonic practice—the back room

---

14. [Two small blocks of stone.—*Trans.*]

of a tavern or aristocratic salon—finally became the Masonic temple that we have known for a little more than two hundred years.

The "tracing board" therefore went from the status of a mental depiction consisting of a symbolic arrangement, which could easily bring to mind a kind of mandala, to that of a veritable architectural blueprint.[15]

But this account—although it is completely pertinent—of the transition from the "tracing board" to the materialized space called the "Masonic temple" remains essentially descriptive and falls well short of what we are hoping for. How does each symbol—including those borrowed from the manual craft of builder or architect—stand out from the others that form the conceptual discourse? What are the possibly comparable laws or paradigms that existed before this style of creation? Can the art of memory, which was simply mentioned in 1599 as possibly contributing to the speculative formation of the plan of the lodge, then the Masonic temple, also help us pierce the "cultural" secret of the way the symbols were formed? What are the historical facts in this regard, and what help do they bring to this hypothesis?

---

15. François Gruson, "Architecture, pensée et action maçonniques," *Ordo Ab Chao*, no. 62 (2011), 170–71.

CHAPTER TWO
The Evolution of
the Art of Memory

To think is to reflect on images.

GIORDANO BRUNO

IT IS SPECIFICALLY within the art of memory that we need to direct our search for the answers to these questions. In the seventeenth century, this extraordinary mnemonic technique, which straddles both analogical thinking and conceptual thought, did not enjoy quite the popularity and efflorescence it had, paradoxically, among those who knew how to read and write in antiquity, as well as during the Middle Ages and the Renaissance.

In antiquity, under the impetus of the first treatises of the *Ad Herennium* and of Cicero, this art was mainly envisioned for use by orators.

During the Latin-influenced Middle Ages, it often continued to serve as an aid for making speeches, but under the pressure of the finest minds and greatest figures of the time, it was naturally integrated into Christian doctrine and its cardinal virtues. After Charlemagne, we find the prestigious names of Albertus Magnus and Saint Thomas associated with it, while the Dominican Order was spreading a domesticated use of it for the purposes of apologetics, conversion, and inquisition. Peter of Ravenna promoted a secular adaptation of this memory technique.

During the Renaissance, while we certainly come across the presence of Erasmus, it is the major figures of Llull,[1] Giulio Camillo, and Giordano Bruno in particular that diverted this art into the mystical, Hermetic direction that would become the major philosophy of that era, while an entire section of the art, primarily dedicated to mnemonic techniques and procedures, remained vital. Frances Yates provides a summary of this under the generic term of the "classical art of memory."

The intellectual and spiritual situation of the art of memory evolved again during the seventeenth century. On the one hand, the importance of the art in accordance with Ramon Llull's definition began to dwindle: eventually all that remained of it with any potency was the search for *the* method.[2] At this same time the upholders of the magical, Hermetic notion of this art had taken possession of the forefront of the stage of ideas—in any case at least since the "revelation" of the writings of Hermes Trismegistus by Isaac Casaubon in 1614. On the other hand, the art was associated with different modes of representing things and ideas, primarily in the development at this time of *emblemata*.[3] These continue to be very poorly understood today, despite the publication of André Alciat's seminal book in Augsburg in 1531.

Seeing the fantastic proliferation of the written and printed word to the detriment of speech memorized by heart and the oral tradition, the Western man of 1700 could have said to himself, as did Victor Hugo (overlooking the anachronistic nature of the quotation in this instance):

---

1. In fact, Frances Yates regards Ramon Llull, who died in 1316, more as a figure of the Renaissance than the Middle Ages; *The Art of Memory*, 176.

2. In my opinion, it is neither neutral nor irrelevant that the year 1637 witnessed the first historical mention of the Mason Word in Scotland (see page 7) and the publication of the *Discourse on Method* by René Descartes. I personally regard this date as an essential milestone in the historical process of the dissociation of thought in the West in its unique and unified form into analogical thought, on the one hand, and conceptual thought, on the other.

3. Cf., mainly Alciat, *Les Emblèmes*.

"This will kill that." Wouldn't it therefore be likely that under these conditions the still-forming Masonic symbolism would become the storage, preservation, and transmission site for a particular form of the art of memory? This was an essentially oral form that was in the midst of being dethroned and swept aside by writing. This is what the historical developments and transformations of the art would seem to suggest, in part.

> *Man cannot understand without images (phantasmata).*
>
> Saint Thomas Aquinas

During the time that spans the end of the sixteenth century and the beginning of the seventeenth century, which is the period that chiefly concerns us here, the importance of the mode of representation in the argument I am making must be emphasized. Alexander Dickson, proponent of Catholicism and defender of Bruno at Oxford in 1584, and whom we see again at the court of King James VI of Scotland in the company of William Schaw (Catholic) and William Fowler (Protestant), published a book on "the shadows." In it he not only discusses the essence of ideas but more particularly "the shadows of ideas." The conversation he recounts between Thamus, the king of Egypt, and Theuth, inventor of art and writing, is insistent "that the invention of writing will not improve memory but destroy it, because the Egyptians will trust in these 'external characters which are not part of themselves,' and this will discourage 'the use of their own memory, within them.' This argument is closely reproduced by Dickson in the conversation of his Thamus and Theutates."[4]

Couldn't we see here precisely, in a belated way certainly, the fallout of the conceptual duopoly between ideas and their expression written by means of letters, which through a natural and mechanical reaction, one could say, would be carving a path that was entirely traced out this

---

4. Yates, *The Art of Memory,* 269.

way to the analogical and reunified formation of the polysemic Masonic symbol?

But if we are to take the Thomist and Dominican concept of the art of memory as truth, then memory will, as Yates points out, retain the *sensibilia* more easily than the *intelligibilia*. Now, if we stick to the evolution (whose broad lines have been rapidly sketched out above) of the historical forms of the art, we must accept the fact that a shift occurred. Originally, the classical concept of the art of memory was given the same status by those living during the midway point of the Middle Ages as that reserved for imagines, *intentiones, res,* and *verba* as symbolic elements intended to occupy the *loci* and to stimulate the memory. During the later period with which we are concerned and which is directly associated with the latter part of William Schaw's life, a transition took place: greater importance was placed on the images (imagines) and the things (res) represented as stimulating factors for memory.

It just so happens that what this shift toward images and materialized representations basically reveals is much more serious and significant than a banal and convoluted scholars' quarrel through the intervention of rival universities (Dickson, Perkins, etc., between 1584 and 1586): it actually concerns the status of the *image*—and images—in the Christian West. The Catholic faith laid claim to it and adapted it, following in the footsteps of the Dominicans of the Middle Ages. The Protestant faith (which in all matters involving the British Isles is a more puritanical expression) rejected it and encouraged iconoclasm. At this same time, Giordano Bruno, far from being tripped up by this apparent contradiction, pushed it even further for his advantage as a complex form of thought in quest of a metaphysical universalism. Frances Yates tells us he was now speaking not of an art but a method: "We institute a method, not about things but about the significance of things."[5]

Far from an elsewhere and nowhere of utopia according to Campanella, wouldn't the future operative and non-operative

---

5. Yates, *The Art of Memory*, 294.

Freemasons of 1600-era Scotland, engaged in an outside of work quest for method but remaining immersed nevertheless in the here and now of spiritually conflictive societies, be in the process of discovering the Masonic symbol beneath the memorized image?

Inasmuch as the purpose of my argument, both now and in 1995, is to prompt a return to original sources, what do I ultimately mean when I speak of Masonic symbols?

If we accept the fact that Masonic symbols were created by their inventors as elements of language and communication intended to transmit moral and spiritual values capable of being made universal, just how did these inventors go about the task they set for themselves?

Their first step was to select the terrain and the domain upon and in which to situate their analogies and metaphors. This would be the domain of the builder in which the "grafting" comes into play, because it naturally combines the master builder (the Great Architect of the Universe), the conceiver of the edifice (the architect), and the worker (the mason on the construction site) in its implementation. The ultimate aim implied by the practices in the field of activity selected this way is well known: in the image of the original temple, the Temple of Solomon, intended to welcome the divine presence among human beings and fix it to one location (the Shekinah). It would consist of building and constructing every edifice naturally capable of permitting the individual to be protected, to live, and to shelter his family, while at the same time building his own self. This spiritual building will thereby ensure the liaison and dialogue between the "little world" that this individual embodies, and the organized "large world" in which he dwells, aware of the favor and good fortune that the Great Organizer will arrange to be his lot in return for his labor, his irreproachable conduct, and his loyalty toward duty.

But the selection of the domain from which the imagery of metaphors can be drawn is not sufficient. The creators of this spiritual and institutional mechanism are going to have to provide this inner architecture of building metaphors with a context and a meaning. Mirroring the role played by intentiones (intentions) and verba (words), in the ancient art of memory, this role would now be played by the human virtues. Through his practice of these virtues the free man would ensure, in the relative sense of social behavior and in the absolute sense of an unattainable *parousia*[6] an advent of the true, the good, and the beautiful into the real time of human life.

Now, with this intentionality, this inner will situated at the origins of the mechanism, we are clearly in the domain of pure, ideal abstraction. What needs to be done to make it so these spiritual intentions and virtues can be transmissible between the generations of elect recipients of this Royal Art of thought and life?

These creators, whose existence I mentioned above and their most likely very advanced state of consciousness, will be impelled to give a tangible body to these spiritual intentions. It will be the images (like the imagines of the art of memory) that are called symbols today, whose role and function are so similar to the ones we find in the works of Llull, Camillo, and Bruno that they are hard to tell apart.

They have to be easily accessible by the intellect (intelligibilia), easily transmissible, and easily made universal (common to all cultural and religious traditions, as the Constitutions of 1723 will recall from the outset). They should finally—and I would add especially—contain within them one trump card. This trump card is that their periodic and repeated evocation by the members of the secret society (whether spoken aloud or written) should ensure that the moral and spiritual value that has been attached to them will immediately and automatically return to the memory of the "follower."

It will escape no one (this is what I wanted to suggest by formulating this hypothesis) that, if this periodic and recurring practice was achieved like a kind of profane liturgy brought into play under the heavy constraint of objectives (the virtues) and means (memorization capable of going as far as their restoration by heart), we are then in the

---

6. [Advent or coming, as in the second coming of Christ.—*Trans.*]

presence of a fairly original creation. This creation is a *ritual* of symbols acted out and reflected within an assembly of Freemasons.

Can a diagram of the creation of our symbols like this—certainly one that was drawn up as a rough outline—and the working of the initiatory transmission, for as much as it appears possible in the eyes of the experts, be reasonably correlated with one or another of the forms that the art of memory has taken over the course of its history? Does the gradual and continuous shift that Frances Yates maintains took place between the end of the Middle Ages and the end of the seventeenth century, from a purely mnemonic technique to one founded on abstractions in which the images and depictions (the numbers, the letters, and the emblems) became predominant, allow us to deduce and state that the source of the symbols of Freemasonry can be found in this new form of the art of memory and in the Hermetic corpus that the great visionaries of that time added on to it? A number of individuals—and not only some minor figures—would certainly put their faith in that belief. However, they never offered any proofs. This is notably the case with Albert Pike, as can be seen in a personal letter he wrote to the historian Robert Freke Gould on January 28, 1888.[7] This is also the impression that David Murray Lyon gives when he writes: "the grafting

---

7. "I have been for some time collecting the old Hermetic and Alchemical works in order to find out what Masonry came into possession of from them. I have ascertained with certainty that the square and compasses, the triangle, the oblong, the three Grand Masters, the idea embodied in the substitute word, the Sun, Moon and Master of the Lodge, and others [were included in the number].

"The symbols that I have spoken of as Hermetic may have been *borrowed* by Hermeticism, but all the same it *had* them, and I do not know where they were used, outside of Hermeticism, until they appeared in Masonry.

"I think that the Philosophers, becoming Free-Masons, introduced into Masonry its symbolism—secret, except among themselves—in the Middle Ages, and not after the decline of operative Masonry began.

"Whoever endowed Masonry with these particular symbols, they were Hermetic symbols; and I know what they meant to the Hermetic writers, French, German, and English. I should think it likely that ASHMOLE became a Mason because others who were Hermeticists had become Masons before him."

of the non-professional element on to the stem of the Operative system of Masonry had its commencement in Scotland probably about the period of the Refomation."[8]

But neither of these authors advances one single persuasive and precise fact that would support this hypothesis. So should we, to the contrary and for all that, attribute any kind of influence in this regard to Bruno and Dickson's adversary on English soil, Pierre de la Ramée, also known as Petrus Ramus (1515–72), whose specific notion, founded on "the method in accordance with dialectical order," was defended mainly by William Perkins of Cambridge? Ramus was a Protestant, a Puritan, and a sympathizer of the iconoclast movement. This fact certainly allowed him to benefit from the very pronounced natural empathy of the intellectual circles of Elizabethan England. But this hostility of his philosophy—and that of his advocate and propagator, Perkins, with respect to images makes it hard to make the real influence he wielded in the period around 1584 compatible with the obscure gestation of Masonic symbolism and its images.[9] Frances Yates provides us with the definitive analysis of this situation:

> The passage is interesting evidence of how the method was developed out of the classical art yet was basically opposed to it on the fundamental point of images. Using the terminology of the classical art, Perkins turns it against the classical art and applies it to the method.[10]

Following an allusion to the poet Philip Sidney, a disciple of John Dee, the great British historian ultimately suggests to us what is a very attractive hypothesis:

---

8. Gould, *A Concise History of Freemasonry,* 340.
9. For more on this, see the remarkable book by René Désaguliers (René Guilly), *Les deux grandes colonnes de la franc-maçonnerie.*
10. Yates, *The Art of Memory,* 276.

In the peculiar circumstances of the English Renaissance, the Hermetic form of the art of memory perhaps goes more underground, becoming associated with secret Catholic sympathies, or with existing secret religious groups, or with incipient Rosicrucianism or Freemasonry.[11]

We can see from that that the best authors were reduced to formulating conjectures that, while they were extremely seductive, never truly managed to come up with the one piece of decisive evidence that would provide us with proof of the direct line of descent we are looking for. It does give us a sure indication that the art of memory, which could have easily served as a matrix for the formation of the Masonic symbols, is to be more obviously sought among its proponents that were "born" in Catholic rather than Protestant milieus. The proof provided by Ramus is clear. But this does not permit us in any way to dispel the amazing paradox that surrounds this obscure birth: the meetings of the first Freemasons—it should be noted that I am not yet speaking of lodges—consisted of *both* Catholics and Protestants, especially Anglicans and Presbyterians. The Jews were not long in joining them in these gatherings. The fact that this took place during a time of terrible war, in which murderous conflicts affected all the religious communities and brought rival and enemy camps into stark opposition, is utterly remarkable. Examination of the history of the other symbolic forms that were also proliferating during this century[12] will not help further our research in this matter. The solution—if there is any solution to be found—will most likely be found somewhere in the neighborhood explored by my original hypothesis: the art of memory—at least its progressive forms over the course of history—has provided the source of the creation of the symbols of Freemasonry. But when has drawing

---

11. Yates, *The Art of Memory*, 286.
12. Most specifically the book on the *emblemata* (emblems) by Alciat, which we briefly looked at on page 14.

from whatever source is available, even analogically, ever been regarded as offering the beginning of proof?

This was the point I had reached not so long ago, nevertheless reassuring myself with the basically reasonable and realistic idea that if nobody had been able to advance even a tiny bit in this direction for more than two centuries, it seems highly unlikely I would succeed where they had failed. But not everything had yet been investigated or said.

CHAPTER THREE

From the Decline of the Image to the Advent of the Letter

Gutenberg's Victory

According to the paradox stated by Husserl, tradition, which is essentially the forgetting of origins, contains within it the articulation of a new life.

EUGENIO GARIN, *HERMÉTISISME ET RENAISSANCE*

AN INSPIRING TEXT that I recently discovered thanks to Claude Gagne,[1] who revealed its existence to me, has today allowed me to dive much deeper into my 1995 hypothesis by contextualizing it in accordance with the insights of an individual who is a recognized authority on the art of memory. This text, which is the work of Madame Claudie Balavoine, an eminent Renaissance researcher and expert, has as its title: "Hiéroglyphes de la mémoire: Émergence et metamorphose

---

1. To whom I would like to pay homage today by dedicating these lines to him.

d'une écriture hiéroglyphique dans les Arts de mémoire du XVIᵉ and du XVIIᵉ siècles" (Hieroglyphs of Memory: Emergence and Transformation of a Hieroglyphic Script in the Arts of Memory during the Sixteenth and Seventeenth Centuries). It was given at a symposium that took place in 1988 that was dedicated to "Hiéroglyphes, langages chiffrés, sens mystérieu au XVIIᵉ siècle" (Hieroglyphs, Coded Languages, Mysterious Meanings in the Seventeenth Century), and published in *XVIIᵉ siècle,* the journal of the Société d'étude du XVIIᵉ siècle (Association of Seventeenth-Century Studies), no. 158 (January–March, 1988).[2]

Because this text is not entirely devoted to the art of memory alone—and to its developments and transitions—but also because it establishes strongly and fittingly the "points of contact" between the old *memoria artificialis,* especially the hieroglyphs,[3] I thought it would be a good idea to now proceed to look at every point raised by Claudie Balavoine in two stages: the explanation of the historic point,[4] then my commentary on the development that can be seen therein.

Point 1: The major development that can be observed is primarily marked by the decline of the meaningful image and the advent of the letter. "The very simultaneity of the enthusiasm they inspired connects both to this transformation of the mental landscape that can be called the Renaissance and what left its mark on the prevailing status of the meaningful image. It will be seen that their dual and joint evolution offers evidence of the gradual decline of the latter toward the end of the sixteenth century and the beginning of the century that followed, as well as the advent of the letter that this decline allowed—a decline

---

2. The content of this text, which is somewhat complex in its formulation, is of such great importance for the understanding of my present argument that I deemed it necessary to reproduce it in its entirety as appendix A in this study.
3. But also, for the sake of completeness, with the "theatrical," the "rebus," the play on words, and so forth.
4. I will indicate that a citation is from the text by Claudie Balavoine whenever I cite it by putting the initials "C. B." at the end of the quote.

that the letter in its turn only accelerated" (C. B.). This insight, which places the emphasis on the considerable transformation introduced by the general spread of printing and the printed text, is certainly not new. But we should note in passing that the fact she places emphasis on the Renaissance should not be viewed by regular and traditional Freemasons casually. Our order was not born in the turmoil and troubles of the eighteenth century, not in the French Revolution—it finds its source of origin in the Renaissance.

Point 2: The rise in power of reason, rationalism, and the utilitarian preeminence of conceptual thought in the West does not give the poet and the philosopher authority to conceal, then destroy the pertinence of the iconic sign. "On the other hand, the classical examples of imagines and the Neoplatonic interpretation of the hieroglyph both converge into a single perception of the *iconic sign* as a concentrated form of meaning and a superior substitute for speech" (C. B.). This convergence that is singled out by our expert as the persistence, despite everything, of the "iconic sign" is of course clearly referring to this other aspect of human thought: analogical thinking. The idea that this proposition contains is, obviously, something that can be found encased in this practical, immediate, and rapid iconic sign, one that we could sum up as ready to use, potentially usable immediately, a portion of meaning and abstract idea that the concepts for which, put into the words of speech, would take much longer to deliver and explain. Beyond the simple role of protection and preservation that this particular form of image fulfills[5] in a broader civilizational context of decline, isn't Madame Balavoine offering us here the beginning of proof that the Masonic symbol in gestation belongs to this attempt of that era to establish a new "superior substitute for speech"?

Point 3: The sign (or the figure, or symbol) loses polysemy and the

---

5. The Freemasons of the Ancient and Accepted Scottish Rite are particularly sensitive to this specific form of symbolism, something that the studies by Monsieur Dominique Jardin on the iconography of the grades tends to take into account.

power of immediate suggestion/signification: "The figure is no longer the generously ambiguous sign of a concept at all but the simple pictorial equivalent of a word: '*dalli quali si cava la parola*' [from which the words were drawn]" (C. B.).

Under the intentionally lapidary name of the figure, Madame Balavoine designates as a positive counterpoint to iconoclasm the principle of all figurations or, to borrow the way Pierre Laurens put it in the reissue of Alciat's work in contemporary style, the symbolic forms. I suggest this interpretation of the text as it is one that does not seem unreasonable to me. It lent support, to a certain extent, to the attempt to secularize artificial memory carried out by Peter of Ravenna and thereby opens, but only in hollow relief, the possibility to create from whole cloth (figurative supports excluded, of course) a new symbolic form of literalness that would not exclude meaning, spiritual abstraction, recourse to the faculty of the imagination, the reminder of moral virtues to which one conformed out of duty and respect for one's given word.

It should be obvious that what I think I see poking out at this stage of the development of the art of memory described by Claudie Balavoine is that the substitute for this weakening practice is the Masonic symbolism created from the tools of the craft, which were able to cross over the now passable threshold framed by the two pillars of the Temple of Solomon.

Point 4: Would the symbolic depiction by the image now be compelled henceforth to bow to the letters and the rules of discourse? The conceptual response from the Renaissance is yes. The analogical response is no.

What has become, during this period of time, of the traditional components of the art of memory, imagines and intentiones, res and verba? "By quickly carving a path this way through the repetitive confusion of the arts of memory, I hope to have strengthened the following connection: as long as the image of the memory, its *imago agens,* was formed almost exclusively around the person, which was the case until the beginning of the sixteenth century, the reference to the hieroglyphs could not find any place. The very terms in which this reference was formulated next show that the prevalence of the human individual as a sign was swiftly rivaled by animals, plants, and the objects of the pseudo-hieroglyphic system revealed during the Renaissance, and that this calling into question seems to have gone hand in hand with the growing assertion that all figurative language, charged as it might be with sacred connotations, could or even should henceforth comply with the rules of discourse. I shall seek to provide proof of this by now studying certain avatars of the *loci* and the *imagines,* in which the *personae* specifically tend to change roles" (C. B.).

The answers to the questions raised by this particular point are now beginning to become discernible. The presence of the individual (the person's imagistic depiction in the art of memory) abandons the field to the benefit of the depiction of the surrounding world: animals, plants, and objects. The idea that the human individual can be the subject of his own building, of his perfectibility, through the memorized reminders connected to his symbolic depiction, gives way. We are moving away from the speculative and mental interiority in which the plan formulated by this "craft of living" (to borrow Cesare Pavese's superb title)[6] consists of making a good man into a better man.

Point 5: In the figurative letters, the depiction of corporeal postures culminates in an alphabet of letters whose purely utilitarian employment henceforth prevails over the representation of the human individual. "These disguised letters therefore originally belonged to the *loci.* The innovation here consists of making certain that they pass alongside the *imagines.* . . . At first glance these letters seem to be strictly obeying the precepts of the *imagines agentes,* to the extent that

---

6. [This book by the great modern Italian writer is customarily translated into English as *This Business of Living.—Trans.*]

they assume ridiculous or obscene positions, but their role is no longer that of *personae* at all. In fact, there is no reason then to wonder about what they are doing or what they might mean, as all they give us to read is the shape of their contortions" (C. B.).

There is also no need to place any added emphasis on this stage of the evolution under study: it speaks sufficiently for itself.

Point 6: Our author now brings up in support of her analysis of the preceding point the peculiar case of the rebus. "The innovation here resides in the henceforth strict application of the rebus principle. It is so rigorously applied it gives the impression that the purpose has been shifted and that the ends have been made subordinate to the means. This is because it is hard to see how the technique of the rebus could be put into general use. The arbitrary nature of its fragmentation specifically makes it hard to memorize, and people can only remember a rebus thanks to its translation, since it can only be read once it has been translated. Of dubious effectiveness on the mnemonic level, the examples of partial rebuses that flourished in the arts of memory reveal just how the game was being played. And didn't they, too, contribute to breaking the *imago* that had reigned since antiquity over the field of memory by stripping it of its proper meaning and replacing it with the rule of the letter and its dizzying combinations?" (C. B.).

This particular example provides a new piece of proof of the general tendency during the seventeenth and eighteenth centuries that sought to relegate the arts of memory and the many uses that had been made of them to a secondary position.

Point 7: Having come to the end of this admittedly fairly general overview, all that remains for Madame Balavoine to do is paint a final portrait of the intellectual and historical conditions that would stand witness to the disappearance of the art of memory in its traditional form. "By drawing away from the theatrical path, by giving a cold shoulder to symbolic figures and turning toward play with letters, the artificial memory was surely responding to the commands of the master encoders of the new times who prescribed a series of trans-positions, the better to scramble the code, but it attracted its decoder, natural memory, into a game that would prove fatal to both of them. This ensured that its only recourse, in this respect, was to vanish.

"I cannot help but be pleased by this suicide of the *Ars memoria* because it offers valuable confirmation of the conclusions I drew, some eight years ago, on the development of the emblematic image during that same era. We can clearly see how interest shifted from the figure to the letter and from the symbol to the word. It was this that was now offered, under a variety of avatars, to curiosity; it was upon this that the ultimate fires of the hieroglyphic mystery were concentrated. Because very little remained of what had been the prac-tice of mnemonic techniques during the heyday of Neoplatonism in the fifteenth century. Caught in the web of the discourse to be memorized, the hieroglyph once again became what it had never truly ceased to be: one scriptural sign among others, albeit one somewhat less popular than the others. Everything fell out as if this new hori-zontal subordination had undone the ancient vertical relationship to Divine Wisdom. Regimented within the Memoria, the fourth part of Rhetoric, it now spoke clearly, and—the ultimate irony—more clearly than the syllables and letters that, during the seventeenth century, irrevocably wrested from it the gift of secrecy" (C. B.).

This says it all—or almost all. For if at this moment the art of memory was doomed to disappear, it was "in this aspect," the aspect of the origins of its creation, that it would later come to be called the *classical* art of memory.

However, a new and original way was soon destined to open for it: speculative Freemasonry and its symbols.

This would be a good time to sum up the historical facts Claudie Balavoine has pointed out and analyzed from the period that is our primary concern: 1583 to 1730. Are the converging lines of these prominent facts of a nature to indicate to us in what sense—as both meaning and direction—the traditional art of memory has evolved?

Is the insertion of this sense into the social and cultural context of Europe in general, and that of the British Isles in particular, then capable of giving us knowledge on the connections that I suggested might exist between the art of memory and the symbolism of the emerging speculative Masonry? Let's examine each of these questions in turn.

Everything indicates that the art of memory reluctantly carried out a considerable transformation of itself, a transformation that ultimately entailed a veritable loss of its sovereignty. It was carried out by the continuous decline of the meaningful image and of writing in images. The imagines evolved toward other forms of pictorial signs, hieroglyphs, rebuses, figurative alphabets, and emblems. One of the consequences of this—and a major one for the argument I am making in this book—is the loss of the theoretical and conceptual value of the figure. Going hand in hand with the abandonment of using locations in a site by nature architectural, we also see the decline of the imagistic representation, and the dramatization and theatricalization of the human persona. Lastly, we see the abandonment of the sign as the "divine vehicle of a divine mystery" (C. B.); what this involves essentially is the loss of the mystery. In conjunction, of course, the crossed destiny drawn up by these developments and shifts leads to what can be described, in the final analysis, as the score of a zero-sum game. Proceeding in correlation with the growing recourse to the common tongue, we witness the irresistible ascension of the letter, the script, and the text. The human body becomes, henceforward, a site, a material that can be shaped and worked, which relegates to a secondary place its natural aptitude for spiritualization (cf. mainly the face as mirror of the soul). And, *last but not least,*[7] our Christianized West announces the glad tidings: the reason of the Cartesian cogito is

---

7. [The italicized text was in English in the original.—*Trans.*]

celebrated as a universal solution (and one that can be universalized) for the problem of the "method," such as it had been posed several centuries earlier by that amazing doctor of the art of memory, Ramon Llull.[8] Poor art of memory! You are nothing more than "Spielerei" [play] (Volkmann)!

8. It can never be repeated too often just what the year 1637 represents in the history of ideas. I repeat, this same year is when the first known mention of the Mason Word appeared in Scotland (Perth), in the poem by Adamson, as well as in the *Discourse on Method* by René Descartes. As a member of the surrealist group in 1964, I can testify that the majority of us at that time considered the publication of Descartes's book as the dire portent of the generalized impoverishment of the human mind and the hegemonic advent of the conceptual rationalist and utilitarian discourse that has been stripped of all its vital, analogical, and imaginary dimensions.

CHAPTER FOUR

The Mason Word as Survival and Renewal of the Ancient Art of Memory

MUST THE ART of memory be forced to resign itself to vanishing, gradually, of course, but irrevocably all the same, given the ascent of writing and the printed book? Must it stop seeking to exercise its empire—and its efficacy—over an imaginary world (that is to say, a real world) that has not yet been disenchanted—a world of a cosmic humanism? Must it yield its place—all of its place—to the reductive anthropology heralded by Descartes in which the world would be henceforth a machine and in which the widespread logic of quantification would be flawlessly applied to a "reality" perceived solely from the angle of reification?

Appearances certainly do not speak in favor of the survival in broad daylight of antiquity's art of memory, and it will not be the twentieth-century procedures of mechanical reproduction—film images, recorded soundtracks, cassette tapes—that, because they are immediately destined for the mass market and stripped of the creative virtues of an individual's spiritual interiority, will offer a subsequent proof to the contrary.

On the other hand, the hypothesis I ventured to advance in 1995, to wit, that the ancient wisdom of the art of the artificial memory will strive to survive, in the increasingly hostile environment of a world that has become disenchanted, by continuing the ideal and spiritual quest of its original procedures, but if I may put it this way, in a "recessed" ["*en creux*"] and clandestine manner. In my opinion, this would be the very innovative project of modern speculative Freemasonry and its symbolic and ritual apparatus.

As a way concretely to shore up this hypothesis, I need only briefly cite the Edinburgh Register House Manuscript (dated 1696, but written earlier), which is both the first known instance of the circulation of the Mason Word and a presumed ad hoc aide-mémoire.[1]

In it the first modern Freemasons describe "the manner of giving the Mason Word." It so happens that this word, the existence of which was revealed for the first time in 1637 (see other mentions in this book) and the substance of it in 1691 (Robert Kirk, manuscript of *The Secret Republic*), because it refers to the two columns of Jachin and Boaz, is consequently clearly alluding to the Temple of Solomon. As Philippe Langlet points out in his book, this architectural metaphor, which we can assess with him as "central," places us from the outset in the traditional perspective of the art of memory in its most classic form. It is also likely that these same Scottish Freemasons had previously informed us of their intentions: "Question: where was the first lodge located? Answer: in the porch of the Temple of Solomon" (*Les Textes fondateurs*, 109).

These "initiates" also described the ceremony for receiving a new brother. The circulation and transmission of the Mason Word are described, as is the handshake, the sign, and the oath. This latter is performed in the presence of—and on—the Bible. This primordial element of the presence of the sacred in a ceremony cannot help but bring to mind the very deeply spiritual and religious rooting of the ancient art. Finally, and as suggested by Philippe Langlet, the fact of locating the

---

1. See the original text that has been expertly translated and presented by Langlet in his book *Les textes fondateurs de la franc-maçonnerie,* 89–121.

key to the lodge "beneath the folds of my liver" is very reminiscent of Saint Augustine and the "various creases and folds" of his memory. The oral tradition could not be made any clearer than when the "tongue" [*la langue*] is explicitly mentioned as being contained "in the bone box."

Could not all of this be considered as part of Masonic ritual? And these earliest Freemasons, who from this date were continuously crafting a symbolism that was mainly founded on the tools of building, would find it quite easy to draw inspiration from the art of memory—and its architectural metaphors—whose existence is mentioned in the Second Schaw Statutes of 1599.

But this "resurgence" of the art of memory in the British secret societies of the seventeenth century appears to me to be taking place, referring now to the spiritual content of the ancient memory, in a clandestine manner as a form of counterpoint. What exactly does this mean?

The ancient art was undone and its prestigious project defeated. The new Europe would be that of the Counter-Reformation and the division of tasks brought about by the advent of the Cartesian model and the scientific method. It would have to adapt to the new conditions imposed on the spirit, and the art of memory, in the new uses and codes that it implements, would have to adapt to this as well.

Internally, the key development in this process would be the decline of the meaningful image to the increasing benefit of the letter. The iconographic representations of objects (to the detriment of the human figure in particular) will be those of the tools of the craft and the furnishings of the lodge, but their ethical and spiritual meanings[2] would now be forced to coexist, for the participants in the ceremony, with the material presence of the tools within the premises. What is thereby lost in clarity on the one side (the abandonment of the inner exploration of the imaginary architectural edifice created by the art of memory) is

---

2. Wasn't one of the oldest definitions of Freemasonry during the eighteenth century "a specific system of morality concealed beneath allegories and illustrated by symbols"?

gained on the other (the material replacing the spiritual, as if in a zero-sum game) in polysemy and poetry. The symbol, both by its pictorial representation and by its clear utterance by means of the oral discourse, would thereby reformulate itself as a new mnemonic code. It would therefore combine—as a concession to the developments of the time—the scientific trappings of rational discourse and the traditional, esoteric significance that, shielded from the founding secret spoken by the Brothers, would allow it to thereby go beyond the profane split between the defenders and the adversaries of the image.[3]

Externally, to the eyes of the surrounding community, the Masonic symbol that was still in the process of being created would be found to satisfy both the divergent postulations of the ancient art and those of the "modern spirit." The crisis of meaning, that to some extent it formed and transported in the thought of these two centuries, would reconcile the reemerging Neoplatonic Hermeticism and the ascendant scientific approach. The feeling of crisis it caused in the effervescent British and French secret societies would be, as shown by the sociologist Michel Maffesoli, the judgment handed down by what is being born over what is dying, through the simple mechanics of saturation. And the new Freemasons would then have an easy task of winning the favor of the Catholics, Protestants, Anglicans, and Jews. A large number of symbols would be borrowed from the Bible (the King James Version of 1604). Their catechisms, which would be "enlightening" for the members and obscure for the profane, would successfully appropriate

---

3. At the very beginning, when the Grand Lodges did not yet exist, when the lodges themselves did not have any fixed locations, when their members were not yet constant and registered, when the place and dates of their meetings were variable and haphazard (often connected to the infrequent desire of the individuals to get together), it was the tracing board, which was drawn on the floor and erased afterward, or even later painted on a canvas, which "took the place" of the imaginary temple of the memory. This is how the act of unrolling and revealing it at the beginning of the session became the essential and founding action. The secrets of the ancient teachings and morals were therefore revealed to those taking part in the meeting, in a repetitive and therefore mnemonic way.

the question-and-response procedures from the most effective recipes offered by the established religions. A very well-known example illustrates this point in a way that is quite obvious. An engraving that is dated from 1754 and carries the title, "A Free Mason form'd out of the materials of his lodge" depicts a humanlike figure with the sun for his head. Both of this figure's arms are squares, and it is holding a compass in its right hand. Its body is formed of a closed book (the Bible) that is topped by a level at the location of the shoulders. The apron it is wearing barely conceals the two globes—one celestial and the other terrestrial. Its legs are the pillars of the temple from which the initials J. and B. [Jachin and Boaz] are absent, and its feet, lastly, indicate 5754–1754.

This could not be made any more obvious for the Freemasons or any more obscure for the profane. Moreover, this engraving is a decorative motif on a water pitcher, for which we have every reason to believe was widely viewed and admired by all during this century. Could these ruses and "precautions" of meaning have been the inspiration that moved David Stevenson when he stated: "To have peopled the lodge of the mind with human images might seem to smack of idolatry both to the Calvinist Masons themselves and to the censorious ministers of the Church of Scotland"?[4] The symbols—those new images—might offer us an answer to this question. It is sufficient in this regard to recall that the first written mention of the image of the "tracing board" as a symbol of the lodge appeared in the Carmick Manuscript of 1727. It says: "This figure represents the lodge."[5] This says it all.

---

4. Stevenson, *The Origins of Freemasonry,* 142–43.
5. Russel, "Le tableau du loge du 1er degree," 14.

CHAPTER FIVE

The Meeting of Conceptual Thought and Analogical Thought

AS I BRING MY CONSIDERATIONS of this topic to a close, I do not believe it would be a complete waste of time to briefly revisit my personal motivation concerning this subject.

The question of the beginnings of our order should be, it seems to me, the subject of a fair and balanced reexamination. This is not because this is a good time to conflate the historical origins and sources. I think in this respect I have clearly drawn the distinction between the two and have given legitimacy to the pertinence of my research by primarily focusing on the question of *intellectual and social sources.* By this I mean the historically documented sources that directly preceded the proto-Masonry and its "dark night," and not, as has been seen, the alleged historical origins that have been situated in the eighteenth century during a period of political and social turmoil that in the realm of ideas was in this instance quite belated (the second half of this century). The period to which I primarily attach myself would be the time that is bounded by two dates: 1583 with the arrival of Giordano Bruno in England, and 1730, in which we see the confirmed appearance of the Hiram-centric legend inside the grade of Master Mason. To truly pin down the ideas, it is necessary to indicate the era during which the upheavals that rocked the reemerging art of memory should not only be grasped as causes (the sources)[1] but as consequence (the gestation of Masonic symbolism),[2] which, I think we can all agree, would easily allow us to describe this situation as complicated.[3]

It would have most likely been helpful to acknowledge the thought of Leibniz (for more, I refer you to the conclusion of the book by Dame Frances Yates on the art of memory) and figurism (for more, see the pertinent presentation given by Pierre Mollier in *Renaissance traditionelle*, nos. 101–2 [January–April 1995]: 88–89). But neither is truly germane to my argument, which carries a dual challenge.

The first challenge was to help demonstrate—even modestly—how much of what touches the history of Freemasonry cannot be validly subtracted from history in general and, more particularly, the history of philosophy in the West. This is all that David Stevenson, who is not a Freemason, and I, who am, have in common. The birth of modern Freemasonry can only be understood, in fact, by placing it back into the larger and more general context of thought that has presided for more than two thousand years, which has been a search for *the method*. This method is what René Descartes would give the impression of having fertilized starting in 1637 by shattering the original unity of thought into conceptual, rational, and quantified thought on the one hand and analogical thought as a storehouse for the ancient traditions on the other. It is not incumbent on Masons alone to take an interest in this aspect of the matter.

The second challenge is more specifically Masonic. It is to

---

1. For more on this refer to footnote 8 at the end of chapter 3.
2. From this point of view, I would like to convey my full gratitude to Madame Claudie Balavoine for having so kindly and graciously granted me permission to reprint her study, from which I have drawn so copiously, as appendix A in this book.
3. If anyone requires further convincing, it should be enough to read the verbatim record of the exchanges between Professor David Stevenson and the member of the Quatuor Coronati Lodge on May 12, 1994, during his interview inside this prestigious lodge of study and research.

demonstrate why speculative Freemasonry is, and has been since the beginning, initiatory by nature. People will object that it is obvious I am wedded to this theory because of my long involvement with the Ancient and Accepted Scottish Rite. I will respond in turn that I do not believe that that is at all true.

Through my own personal inner practice and my initiatory convictions shared with other men whose own choices have sent them here, I now know how to gain access to certain states of Being and, sometimes, to the meanings that are hidden from our world that we label as real. I believe I can also say, like Rudyard Kipling in "The Palace:"

After me cometh a Builder. Tell him, I too have known.

I also know how to say, as did the Roman sages: *Festina lente.*[4]

So now, how can we summarize the stages and the progression of the hypothesis that I shored up with the help of the remarkable books by three non-Mason academics and historians?

In 1995, I suggested that by cross-checking the facts put forth by Dame Frances Yates and Professor David Stevenson, it would be possible to infer that the classical art of memory, which was practiced during the late Renaissance in the British Isles, was a major source that directly influenced the structuring of the mechanisms of the initiatory transmission of the then emerging speculative Freemasonry.

Then, in 2011, now supporting my conjectures on the emergence and transformation of a hieroglyphic writing in the art of memory described and analyzed by Claudie Balavoine, I was able to additionally suggest that the belated withering of the art of memory, far from leading to its utter disappearance, had in some way unintentionally ensured its survival in another form, Masonic symbolism was still in the process of being created, thereby de facto making sport of the conflict that

---

4. [*Festina lente* was a motto adopted by both the emperors Augustus and Titus (and borrowed by the Medicis centuries later). It means "Make haste slowly." —*Trans.*]

placed Catholics and Protestants in opposition on the field of their bellicose controversies regarding the image, the word, and the sign.

With this point established, would it now be possible to consider the year 1637 as a marker dating the end of the search by European consciousness for a unique and unified method that would force the philosophers and poets, the scientists and artists, and the "geometers" and the clergymen to choose between the mathematical and utilitarian rationalism of conceptual thought on the one hand and the symbolic and imagistic language of analogical thought on the other? As noted above, there is support for advancing this hypothesis, since it was in 1637 that we see the publication of the *Discourse on Method* by René Descartes, as well as the first confirmed written occurrence of the existence of the "Mason Word" in Perth, Scotland, in a Rosicrucian context.

But shouldn't we go further and at this same time advance the hypothesis that this Masonic symbolism still in the course of being formed would henceforth bring together conceptual thought and analogical thought for the practitioners of the Masonic method? And could this reconciliation be carried out in the context of a European consciousness that had lost the reference points of a thought that had not been divided, which was now abandoning itself to the spiritual decadence of a Western society that was becoming inexorably technical, quantitative, and commercial?

Therefore, perhaps it is not so unseemly to put forth the notion that the creation of Masonic symbolism that was being carried out around 1637 was done so through transformation of the art of memory and the grafting of a post-Renaissance Hermeticism on the professional milieu of the "craft" in Scotland? *Who knows?*[5]

---

5. [In English in the original text—*Trans.*]

APPENDIX A

Hieroglyphs of Memory

*Emergence and Transformation of
a Hieroglyphic Script in the Arts of
Memory during the Sixteenth and
Seventeenth Centuries*

By Claudie Balavoine

THE LINK THAT FORMS the conjunction here is not the arbitrary fruit of a forced encounter between research conducted elsewhere on the memoria artificialis and the subject of this symposium. There are numerous points of contact between this sacred script, which had been an emotionally riveting factor since the beginning of the fifteenth century, and this intellectual function, which became a subject of concern at the same time when it had become necessary to shore up this rediscovered art with regulations.[1] The very simultaneity of

This article was published in *XVIIᵉ siècle,* no. 158 (January–March 1988): 51–68, a journal published by the Society for Seventeenth-Century Studies with the support of the CNL, the CNRS, and the City of Paris; the issue includes the proceedings from a symposium called "Hieroglyphs, Coded Languages, Mysterious Meanings in the Seventeenth Century."
1. Italy was ahead of everyone here, as it was in other things, by a good half century. Florentine circles became immediately infatuated with the manuscript of Horapollo

the enthusiasm they inspired connects both to this transformation of the mental landscape that can be called the Renaissance and what left its mark on the prevailing status of the meaningful image. It will be seen that their dual and joint evolution offers evidence of the gradual decline of the latter toward the end of the sixteenth century and the beginning of the century that followed, as well as the advent of the letter that this decline allowed—a decline that the letter in its turn only accelerated.

It was inevitable that these two different languages would eventually cross paths. On the one hand, both were part of an architectural site. Since the time of antiquity, it was said repeatedly that the artificial memory was a writing in images whose support was an architecture in the mind and not wax or paper: *"Loci cerare aut chartae simillimi sunt, imagines, litteris, disposition et collocatio imaginum scripturae pronuntiatio lectioni."*[2] For their part, the testimonies of a Lucan or an Ammianus Marcellinus, the contemplation of the obelisks that had wound up in Rome, showed that hieroglyphic writing was inscribed by images placed on sites of stone;[3] and this is something Francesco Colonna had clearly grasped, although he simply interpreted, invented, or reinvented *inscriptions.*

It was this monumental script that Leon Battista Alberti coveted

---

(*continued from p. 41*) brought back by Christoforo Buondelmonti. See Karl Giehlow, "Die Hieroglyphenkunde des Humanismus in der Allegorie der renaissance . . . ," in *Jahrbuch der Kunsthistorischeb Sammlungen in Wien*, XXXII, 1 (Vienna and Leipzig, 1915), and E. Iverson, *The Myth of Ancient Egypt and Its Hieroglyphs* (Copenhagen, 1961). Francesco Colonna, who wrote *Hypnerotomachia Poliphili: The Strife of Love in a Dream* around 1460 and most likely never knew of the existence of this work, offers evidence of the revolutionary interest in hieroglyphic writing, for which he provides some fascinating counterfeits. For more on the arts of memory during the end of the Middle Ages, see Paolo Rossi, "Imagini e memoria locale nei secoli XVI–XVᵉ," vol. 2, 1958, 149–91.

2. The *Rhetorica ad Herennium* (*Rhetoric for Herennius*), III, XXI–30; Cicero cites the testimonies of Charmadas and of Metrodorus of Scepsis: *"quorum uterque tanquam litteris in cera, sic se aiebat imaginibus in iis locis quos haberet, quae meminisse vellet perscribere"* (*De oratore* II, 360).

3. See Lucan, III, 224; Ammianus Marcellinus, XVIII, 8–10, etc.

specifically for its triumph over time, and he advised it for those memorial constructions known as tombs.[4] Similarly the arts of memory in the fifteenth century arranged for the insertion of the *imagines* in the monumental loci that, fictional as they might be, were nevertheless fully capable of repelling the attacks of time through constant rememorizing.[5]

On the other hand, the classical examples of the *imagines* and the Neoplatonic interpretation of the hieroglyph both converge into a single perception of the *iconic sign* as a concentrated form of meaning and a superior substitute for speech. Is the *Rhetoric for Herennius,* when it proposes summarizing all the circumstances of a trial with a single image that would then be capable of giving back all the different knowledge with which it is pregnant to whoever knows how to read it, fundamentally different from the one whose dazzling intuition was admired by Marsilio Ficino?[6]

The affinities of these two translations into images could not fail to be pointed out during the Renaissance. I will therefore seek to identify

---

4. Alberti, *De re aedificatoria,* VIII, 4, with respect to tombs: "Our ancestors would gild their letters onto marble with bronze. The Egyptians employed the following sign language: a god was represented by an eye, Nature by a vulture, a king by a bee, time by a circle, peace by an ox, and so on. They maintained that each nation knew only its own alphabet, and that eventually all knowledge of it would be lost—as has happened with our own Etruscan." Leon Battista Alberti, *On the Art of Building in Ten Books,* translated by Joseph Rykwert, Neal Leach, and Robert Tavernor (Cambridge: MIT Press, 1988) 256. For more, see my article, "Le modèle hiéroglyphique à la Renaissance," in Lafond et al., *Le Modèle à la Renaissance* (Paris: Éditions Vrin, 1986), 216ff.

5. Peter of Ravenna, in his *Phoenix sive de artificiosa memoria* (Venice, 1491), recommended churches for this purpose and is said to have set up hundreds of thousands of this type during his travels.

6. See the *Rhetoric for Herennius,* III, XX–33: "And we shall place the defendant at the bedside, holding in his right hand a cup, in his left, tablets, and on the fourth finger, a ram's testicles. In this way we can have in memory the man who was poisoned, the witnesses, and the inheritance." (For an explanation of the details, see Yates, *The Art of Memory,* 11). Ficino, echoing Plotinus, defines hieroglyphs as follows: "Egyptian priests, in order to signify divine objects, did not employ letters but complete figures of plants, trees, and animals, because God most likely has an awareness of things that is not a complete and discursive philosophy but their simple and direct form." (Translated by André Chastel in *Opera Omnia,* II, 1768).

beforehand the moments and modalities that were very quickly established between both of them. Then the very orientation of these comparisons will be used to guide our attempt to grasp the evolution of this new "hieroglyphic" language that the arts of memory were promoting. Our primary interest throughout this study is focused on the strictly linguistic aspect of this style of hieroglyphic translation, leaving to Frances Yates and her disciples the already thoroughly cleared fields of their philosophical and magical meanings.[7] Until the present time, the technical aspect of the *Artes memoriae* has only earned the derision of researchers. The pioneer of these researchers, Ludwig Volkmann, deemed all their refinements as futile and saw in these arts nothing but Spielerei.[8] It so happens that the strategy of the memory could not help but be narrowly dependent on the representational system of a given era and its customary forms of expression. If the arts of memory that would be used here are sometimes devoid of any intrinsic theoretical value, the light they cast on things is not negligible. Through them, if we take the trouble to interrogate the sometimes miniscule variations of their precepts, we can read an evolution—and maybe even a revolution—in the very concept of coding, and the reciprocal play of the image and the letter.[9]

TOWARD A HIEROGLYPHIC WRITING

The splendid book by Frances Yates has made the use of loci and imagines in the practice of memorizing familiar to everyone. It is, however,

---

7. See her book *The Art of Memory.* This is why the extremely important contribution of Giordano Bruno will be deliberately omitted although this man wrote several different arts of memory toward the end of the sixteenth century.

8. Ludwig Volkmann, "Ars memorativa," in *Jahrbuch der Kunsthistorischeb Sammlungen in Wien,* special edition 30 (Vienna, 1929), 111–203.

9. There is a chronological restriction to be added to the one I have already imposed on my subject. My material does not allow me to advance very far into the seventeenth century. The evolution I am seeking to describe here took place in the last quarter of the sixteenth century and the first quarter of the seventeenth century. But the very way the invention of later arts of memory ran dry corroborates the conclusions that suggest what they were and became during an earlier time.

essential that my argument open with a strict definition of the original value of the expression of the *imagines agentes*, which are constantly recurring through the history of this topic, but subject to disparities, if not to say misfortunes, in which the transformation I am seeking to update was at play. To do this, we shall refer back to such fundamental texts as the *Rhetoric for Herennius, On Oratory*, and the *Institutes of Oratory*.

Cicero uses the expression in a passage from *On Oratory*, one which Quintilian also cited earlier as a fundamental text on artificial memory and was subsequently often repeated. It is not one I could dispense with to make my case: "*Locis est utendum multis, inlustribus, explicatis, modicis intervallis; imaginibus autem agentibus, acribus, insignitis, quae occurrere celeriterque percutere animum possint.*" I would like to translate it this way, with some glosses:

> Numerous places should be employed; they must be clear and defined, and spaced apart from each other at moderate intervals; and images (I would rather say "figures") that are fully active and striking, and stamped with a distinctive sign that is capable of immediately presenting itself to the mind and leaving a strong impression.

Agere, which is employed here in the absolute sense, can with some difficulty be given the meaning of "prominent" or "projecting" ["*saillant*"].[10] On the other hand, there is ample confirmation of its use in theatrical language, in which it means "playing a role." We should carefully examine the examples provided by *Rhetoric for Herennius;* this will let us see that the theater plays a major role therein.[11] We could multiply the arguments in favor of a strictly theatrical notion of the

10. *De oratore*, II, 358. Daniel Arasse, responsible for the French translation of *The Art of Memory*, made the mistake of incorrectly copying here the mistranslation of the Budé edition, "*images saillants,*" [prominent or protruding images], imparting an error to Frances Yates that she avoided making: "and images which are active" (23).
11. *Ad Herenium*, III, XXI–34. The text suggests, in fact, if we take the verse *Iam domum itionem reges Atrides parant*, presenting one part as "Domitius raising his

memory among Latin authors, but my intention is not to reconstruct how the *Ars memorativa* functioned in antiquity here. This return to the source is simply aiming to posit that, in these Latin texts that served as a foundation for all that was constructed later, the image of memory first had a person, whose possible posture and accessories carried the meaning that was to be memorized.

Personae

The Middle Ages were quite familiar with the *Rhetoric for Herennius,* which was all the more popular as it was then attributed to Cicero.[12] The generous use it made of individuals to inhabit such sacred places as Paradise, Purgatory, and Hell and the systematic allegorization to which it subjected the vices and virtues, especially in this context, demonstrates that the lesson drawn from this text clearly confers the essential role to the personae. Tradition and a return to sources worked together therefore to ensure the revitalization of the *Ars memorativa* that arose from these elements in the fifteenth century.

This is exactly what happened. Peter of Ravenna in his famous *Phoenix,* whose first edition was published in 1491,[13] advised his readers to populate the localities with beautiful women. For example, in order to remember *panem* [bread], it would be necessary to place a *puellam*

(*continued from p. 45*) hands to heaven while he is whipped by the Marcii Reges" (for *Iam domum itionem reges*), then "Aesopus and Cimber being dressed as for the roles of Agamemnon and Menelaus in Iphegenia" (for *Atrides parant*).

12. This mistaken attribution persisted until the end of the sixteenth century, although it had already been condemned earlier by Lorenzo Valla.

13. This book would be continually republished over the sixteenth and seventeenth centuries. But it is plausible that during this latter era these publications had a more archaeological than pragmatic value. This was also the time when people were seeking to tote up all the acquisitions of the Renaissance, hence the glut of dictionaries, directories, and collections; proof, in fact, that what was being collected had become sterile to a certain degree and was seen more as an object of curiosity rather than a tool that was still functional. For the arts of memory, I can cite the *Variorum de arte memoriae tractatus sex* (Frankfurt, 1678), which was a collection of treatises dating from the beginning of the seventeenth century. We will revisit this point.

nudam [nude girl] in the site (to remember the singular) who was touching a loaf of bread with one foot (for the accusative). It is easy to see how the application of the most banal object of the theatrical principle was incompatible with a hieroglyphic conception of the artificial memory. Far from providing that condensation of speech for which the *Rhetoric for Herennius* offered an example, the obsession for staging, supposed to be the sole thing to have an impact on the imaginative faculty, diluted the smallest word into an iconic complexity that led to the opposite of the shortcut achieved by the ideogrammatic hieroglyph as conceived by Florentine Neoplatonism. Furthermore, the entire human body had hardly any right to citizenship in these *Hieroglyphica* of Horapollo that consistently served the Renaissance as its unique and necessary reference when it came to hieroglyphs. So there is no cause for surprise that, although this decoding text had been known since 1419 and immediately studied in Italy, and although the art of memory was, without any continuous solution, defined as a script that used images instead of the letters of the alphabet, this mnemonic technique would not be compared with hieroglyphic writing until the sixteenth century. Peter of Ravenna, when dedicating an edition of his *Phoenix* to Conrad Peutinger, the well-known connoisseur of Horapollo's *Hieroglyphica*, made no allusion to this kind of writing.[14] In 1508, Thomas Murner defended his method that allowed his students to "gain knowledge quite quickly by casting a simple glance over the cards as if they were consulting a book, which was so effective that they managed to almost use images as letters of the alphabet." He, too, did not establish any comparison.[15] However, the hieroglyph was not slow in nominally entering the stage.

---

14. See Volkmann, "Ars memorativa," 146.
15. Thomas Murner, *Logica Memorativa* (Strasbourg, 1508), *Modus practicandi*: "*qui ex simplici chartarum intuitu mox in imaginibus quasi in libris recensebant etiam promptissime u fere pro litteris imaginibus uterentur.*"

THE HIEROGLYPHIC REFERENCE

In 1523, in a book cited by Ludwig Volkmann, *Ein kurzer Bericht wie man die Gedächtnis wunderbar versterken kann*, Lorenz Friesen advises his readers to mentally translate "white" as "snow," "fear" by "hare," while referring explicitly to the ancient Egyptians and counseling the student to practice by studying Horapollo.[16] Fifty years later, Cosmas Rossellius, to whom is owed one of the most heavily used treatises, the *Thesaurus artificiosae memoriæ*, published in Venice in 1579, discusses Egyptian hieroglyphs at length. But using the ancient testimonies of Diodorus, Lucan, Apuleius, and Macrobius as support, he strove to prove that these "Egyptian letters" were primarily intended to express concepts and they should in no way be confused for letters of the alphabet.[17] The list of equivalencies he subsequently provided confirms this notion of the hieroglyph as ideogram, which conforms in every point with the official position on the Egyptian question.[18]

A fairly radical turning point took place at the end of the century. In his *Plutosofia,* which appeared in Padua in 1592, Brother Philippo Gesualdo no longer considered "hieroglyphs" to be a specific case of memorization through figures. This indirect style of mnemonic inscription—because he conceived of an immediate style of inscription at the same time, a point we shall revisit—became conflated with the hieroglyphic practice for him. This is a strange merger in which the classical comparison of the memorized image with the alphabetic written form (*come il luogo e assomigliato alla carta, cosi l'immagine*

---

16. Volkmann, "Ars memorativa," 163.

17. II, VIII, 119: "*Hoc autem dixerim ut nemo existimet huiusmodi notae Aegyptiorum pro literis, sed pro conceptus mentis explicantibus poni posse. Ideo ab illis non literae sed hiroglyphicae literae dictae sunt.*"

18. This same orientation can be seen in the work of Giambattista della Porta, who devoted chapter 18 of his *Ars reminiscendi* to hieroglyphs. This book was published in Naples in 1602 but appeared in Italian in 1556: "Quomodo per hieroglyphica Aegyptiorum memoriae subveniatur." This is followed by a packed list of four pages of "hieroglyphic" equivalencies based on the work of Valeriano, who practically retained only animals as signs.

e corrispondente alla scrittura distesa nella carta) is taken literally and in which, in a symmetrical movement, the hieroglyph comes down from its ideogrammatic throne to transform into a simple graphic sign. Therefore one writes: *"con figure ieroglifiche dalle quali si cava la parola, come facevano gli Egitti,"* and the examples cited next leave no doubt as to the henceforth accepted equivalence of *"figure ieroglifiche"* and *"parola"*: *"Liquali, sia per esempio, per questa furore scrivevano un leone, per il pigro, un camelo, per la terra, un bue, per la fortezza, la parte anteriore d'un leone e cosi dell'altri ieroglifichi liquali per via conditione naturale rappresentavano quelle parole."*[19]

The figure is no longer the sign at all. At the moment when the excessive sacralization of the monumental Egyptian script still formed an unyielding barrier to its decoding, the arts of memory that transformed their initiate into an encryptor treated the hieroglyph as a simple writing tool.[20] This could not help but do harm to the sacred nature that had been imparted to it. Gesualdo actually, after returning several pages later to *questo modo che usavanno gli Egitti, liquali invece di lettere e parole dipingevanno animali, pietre, herbe et simili,* provides an example that strikes a rude blow against the dual deification of hieroglyphic writing, which Neoplatonism perceived as the divine vehicle of a divine mystery. In fact, he proposed to hieroglyphically retain *servus fidelis* and *prudens*. To accomplish this he put in the locality a *servus* known to him, who was holding a dog on a leash (fidelis) in one hand and with the other making the sign of leaping on a snake (prudens). The anomaly, which is, incidentally, completely relative for an art of memory, is not taking the place of a mystery here.[21] Mystery is as absent from the sign as from what it signifies.

Johannes Austriacus, whose *De memoria artificiosa libellus* appeared

---

19. Page 31 (C.B.). The italics are mine.
20. For more on the bestowal of a sacred nature, see page 43, note 4, on Alberti.
21. We know that all the authors, in fact, prescribe oddity.

in Strasbourg in 1603, fits into this same lineage. The chapter he devotes to hieroglyphs clearly places the emphasis, as is shown by its title, *De scriptura hieroglyphica*. After reminding his readers that the Egyptians used hieroglyphs to express ideas, he attributes to these latter a literary value, in the same way: "Because the letters of the alphabet, which had not yet been invented, were not available to them, they used things to express *ideas as well as to form letters and words*."[22]

In the version that Adrian Le Cuirot provided of Lambert Schenkel's rules of memory in 1623, titled *The Storehouse of the Sciences or the True Art of Memory*, the same tendency is verified: "[One shall also proceed] similarly by signifying what is represented, as the Egyptians did *for letters and elocutions*, by painting animals, herbs, and plants, which signified the property most appropriate to them, like haughtiness was represented by a peacock, and a tortoise would demonstrate laziness."[23]

By quickly carving a path this way through the repetitive confusion of the arts of memory, I hope to have strengthened the following connection: as long as the image of the memory, its *imago agens*, was formed almost exclusively around the person, which was the case until the beginning of the sixteenth century, the reference to the hieroglyphs could not find any place. The very terms in which this reference was formulated next show that the prevalence of the human individual as a sign was swiftly rivaled by animals, plants, and the objects of the pseudo-hieroglyphic system revealed during the Renaissance, and that this calling into question seems to have gone hand in hand with the growing assertion that all figurative language, charged as it might be with sacred connotations, could or even should henceforth comply with the rules of discourse. I shall seek to provide

---

22. "*Cum literis tum nondum inventis carerent, rebus Et ad exprimendos animi conceptus Et ad literas dicionesque formandas utebantur*." The italics are mine.
23. Adrian Le Cuirot, *Le Magazin des sciences ou vray art de la mémoire* (Paris, 1623); see Lambert Schenkel, *Gazophylacium* (Strasbourg, 1610). The italics are mine.

proof of this by now studying certain avatars of the loci and the imagines, in which the personae specifically tend to change roles.

WHERE THE BODY BECOMES A LOCALE

Trying to identify this change compels us to give priority, in the sequence of the Renaissance memory arts, to any innovation, no matter how futile or aberrant it might appear to us. It is of course understood that the ancient concept of essentially architectural places and essentially theatrical images persisted through the centuries, or at least was scrupulously held in mind. But while the ancient texts accepted the natural site in a pinch (we know that Metrodorus of Scepsis had the signs of the zodiac), they never suggested that the human body could, if I might say so, take its place. The Middle Ages would divvy up the heavens as it pleased, and organize Paradise, Purgatory, and Hell, but would not make any strictly topographical use of the body. It so happens that at the end of the sixteenth century, the whole body or the hand alone became the favored site for mnemonic inscriptions.

THE MAP OF THE BODY

Cosma Rosselio (also known as Cosmas Rossellius), in his *Thesaurus artificiosae memoriæ* (1579), sacrificed to earlier notions of the loci. In his work we find again Paradise, Purgatory, and Hell, and he proposes, like Peter of Ravenna, to manufacture architectural locales in churches and abbeys. But he also suggests the use of alphabetical series of philosophers, poets, craftsmen, and so forth, each of which would furnish a site on which subsidiary images could be inscribed. To do this, he counted forty-one secondary sites on the anatomical surface, and was able to add another twenty-eight, by penetrating inside the body (see figs. 1 and 2).[24]

---

24. Of the twenty-odd engravings in the book, seven are devoted to the body and five to the hand, an indication, in my opinion, of a conscious innovation.

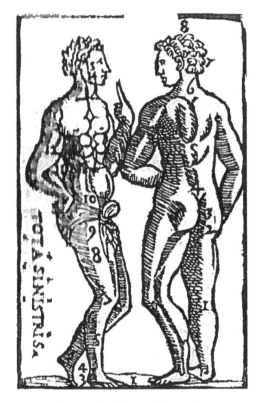

Figure 1. Cosma Rosselio,
Thesaurus artificiosae memoriae, 1579.

Gesualdo, in his *Plutosofia* (1592), is satisfied with forty-two secondary locales, to be traveled through in the direction of the reading. One starts at the right foot and climbs up to the head, and then goes back down the body to the left foot (the right foot being located on the left of the image). One engraving shows a naked body whose parts, scrupulously numbered, demarcate the mental path (fig. 3, on page 54).[25] Of bodies in action in audacious postures, of those living persons that Peter of Ravenna wished to be pretty women suitable to excite the

---

25. Except for a basic architectural blueprint, this is even the only illustration in the treatise.

Figure 2. Cosma Rosselio,
Thesaurus artificiosae memoriae, 1579.

memory, there remains only an anemic chart. But he goes even further because he concludes from this that a locale like this cannot receive the classical imagines without impropriety *se no per forza de fantasia* [if not by means of fantasy]. Here is where we see the corollary of this new mnemonic topography looming: the concomitant image transformation of the *imago* that will be discussed later.

Francesco Panigarola, whose treatise on memory appeared in French in 1604, proposed a kind of mixed system consisting of ten cities, to be memorized in a set order, for example, in alphabetical order, each of which could offer a memory, and in an equally immutable order, ten similar people, of both sexes and distinct ages. He

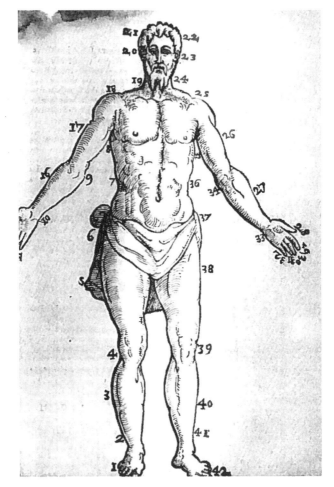

Figure 3. Filippo Gesualdo, *Plutosofia*, 1592.

said, "it is necessary that you imagine them naked so as to be able to clothe and decorate them with all the things that should be used for figures."[26] Nothing could better illustrate the fact that the peo-

---

26. *L'art de prescher et bien faire un sermon avec la Mémoire locale et artificielle,* created by the Reverend Father François Panigarole and translated by Gabriel Chappuis (Paris, 1604), 74. For Frances Yates, this Dominican "is an example of the enfeeblement of the art since its great era in the Middle Ages, exhibiting the kind of mentality which is to be found in the late memory treatises" (*The Art of Memory*, 246). Please permit me to overlook this value judgment in order to concentrate on this "kind of mentality."

ple are now of no importance. Moreover, in order to "erase the text," Panigarola proposes to "race over the empty places or else to discuss the naked [persons] two or three times." *The Storehouse of the Sciences* validates this new concept but does so, however, by sacrificing to proper decorum. The personages that obligingly lend themselves to the function of place are decently clothed. It follows that the body is no longer as easily cut into many pieces. It is now only subdivided into five secondary sites, marked by small tablets set underneath the right foot, then in the right hand, over the head, in the left hand, and under the left foot (fig. 4).

Figure 4. Adrian Le Cuirot,
The Storehouse of the Sciences, 1623.

THE MARKED HAND

The hand has always been used to support memory.[27] But this ancillary role cannot be compared to the methodical chart of a terrifyingly abstract complexity that was drawn up at the very beginning of the seventeenth century by the Calabrian monk Giralamo Marafioti in his *De Arte reminiscentiae.* This work may appear strange and impractical to us, but it must have corresponded to the tastes of the time since it was published at least five times in the first quarter of the seventeenth century.[28] While simultaneously offering instruction in the classical art, Marafioti suggested using the four surfaces of both hands as locales (see fig. 5). He distinguished as specific places the phalanges and mounts of the fingers, as there are twenty-three in each hand (the number of letters in the alphabet, Marafioti hastens to point out). This all forms a whole of ninety-two sites, which can be infinitely multiplied by placing the hands in different positions or by coloring them. Each secondary site is characterized by a particular symbol—moon, circle, triangle, ring—which could indeed appear remotely hieroglyphic but which in fact is meaningless.[29]

At the beginning of the seventeenth century, Lambert Schenkel proposed using the hands as secondary sites, arranged in accordance with the traditional *M* to mark the four corners and the center, and intended

---

27. As early as the eleventh century, Guido d'Arezzo was using the "harmonic hand" as a memory aid. Its use continued into the eighteenth century. See J. Smits van Waesberghe, *Musikerzeihung: Lehre und Theorie der Musik im Mittelalter,* Leipzig: VEB Deutscher Verlag fur Musik, 1969. We are familiar with the methods for computing calendars in antiquity, which were readopted for use in the Middle Ages. See Pierre Riche, *Écoles et enseignement dans le Haut Moyen Âge,* Paris: Aubier, 1979, 227. In his *Ludus Studentium Friburgensium* (1511) Murner also suggests the use of a hand on which the letters of the alphabet have been written to remember the rules of prosody.

28. *De arte reminiscentiae per loca et imagines, ac per notas et figuras in manibus positas,* published in Frankfurt, 1602; Strasbourg, 1603; and Venice, 1605, 1615, and 1624.

29. I do not deny the possibility here of an alchemical reference, but it would not weaken the argument I am making.

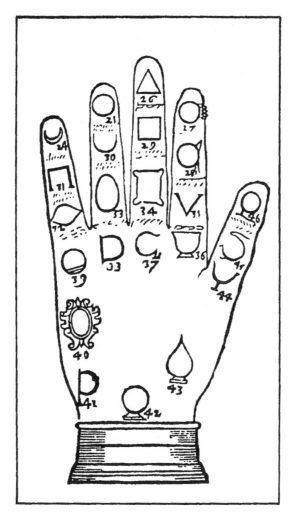

Figure 5. Giralamo Marafioti,
De Arte reminiscentiae, 1602.

to multiply the wall surfaces of classical architectural sites (fig. 6, on page 58). Here again, the choice of script and the *locus memoriae* has heavy repercussions on the very letters of the script. But before we enter into a discussion on the parallel avatars of the *imagines memoriae,* please indulge me in a momentary *excursus* while I make the connection between this emergence of the body transformed into a memory site and a contemporary phenomenon: a renewed taste for physiognomy.

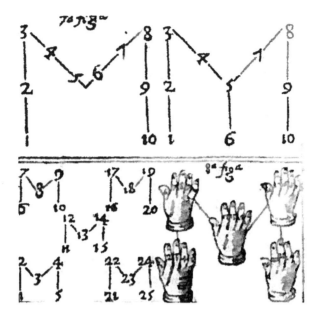

Figure 6. Adrian Le Cuirot,
The Storehouse of the Sciences, 1623.

PHYSIOGNOMIC HIEROGLYPHS

It is undeniable that toward the end of the sixteenth century people were searching the body for markings or inscriptions. This curiosity is proven by the numerous reprintings of the *Physiognomonia* by Giambattista della Porta, who was also the author—which may not be a simple coincidence—of an art of memory.[30] The fact that its content was hardly new and made abundant use of Aristotle, Polemon, and Adamantius, should not concern us here. We should simply focus on the perspective that this revived interest implies. It would seem to me that this way of reading the body finds its reflection—which is reversed

---

30. Giambattista della Porta's *De humana Physiognomonia libri IV* (Sorrento, 1586), translated by the author into Italian, would appear in dozens of editions during the first half of the seventeenth century. Della Porta was also published in Naples in 1677: *Della Chirofisionomia overo di quella parte della humana Fisionomia che si appartiene alla mano . . . tradotti da un manoscritto latino.*

like all reflections—in the writing on the body advocated by Rosselio, Marafioti, and Schenkel. In both cases, in fact, the face or the hand are mere locations for inscriptions and readings/writings and have no meaning in and of themselves. They are devoid of any movement and gestural expression. They simply lie flat. The lines of the hand and the features of the face precisely play the role of writing on a surface.[31] The moral character is written in curves, bumps, and angles that are sometimes highlighted by some color. Here we have a strong impression of again witnessing a kind of dematerialization of the hieroglyphic sign. At first glance, the animal heads that della Porta drew himself and connected with famous portraits, seem to fit into the emblematic tradition. But the trail leads us astray. It is no longer the nature of the lion or the swine that matters, and even less the habit of the one to tear its young to pieces or the power of the other to send an elephant fleeing (upon which Horapollo based some of his interpretations[32]), but the sign "powerful extremity" or "thick lips," which, carrying a definite meaning, could be combined with others to write out the character of a given individual.

The rebirth of physiognomy and one of its components, that *chirofisonomia* that della Porta was keen on not seeing confused with chiromancy,[33] thereby corroborates the new importance granted at the same time to the sites of corporeal memory. Furthermore, this way of making the face or the hand a set of abstract symbols is surprisingly evocative of the system of literal inscriptions that the arts of memory had been increasingly advocating as similar supports.

---

31. Let's say, to be exact, it is a kind of writing in relief, but the memorization is also done in three dimensions.

32. Horapollo, *Hieroglyphica,* respectively, II, 38 (for great wrath) and II, 86 (for the gossipy man who sends the king fleeing).

33. Rejecting the prophetic dimension is not simply an oratorical precaution for him. What is involved here in fact is a change of attitude with respect to the "sign" that no longer refers to a divine will (the fate of the individual), but to a reality (his character).

FROM THE IMAGE TO THE LETTER

The hieroglyphic reference in the arts of memory had already had an effect, as we have seen, of incorporating the image into the letter. This tendency is confirmed by the inexorable seizure of the domain of the image by the letter, which takes place in three stages and on three levels: the extremely precocious emergence of figurative alphabets, the extension of the rebus, and finally what its authors themselves called direct inscription.

The Figurative Alphabets

Giving each letter of the alphabet a figurative appearance is not a later invention. The *Ars memorativa* by Jacobo Publicius, published after the *Oratoriae artis epitome* in Venice in 1482 (but known since 1460) already offered an alphabet in which each letter was depicted by an object that resembled it, *A* by a compass or ladder, *B* by a lute, and so on, and Cosma Rosselio only amplified this direction (fig. 7), which is also the case with an alphabet in which each letter is intended to be deduced by the initial of the name of an animal. But make no mistake: for Publicius, this only served as a simple way to demarcate the places, the *locorum notatio,* in order to make it easier to navigate them without the risk of missing the *ordo locorum,* the fundamental rule of mnemonic inscription. These disguised letters therefore originally belonged to the loci. The innovation here consists of making certain that they pass alongside the imagines.

The alphabets of Publicius would be subsequently picked up by others and completed. Cosma Rosselio would add a description of an alphabet of human postures, for which della Porta would later give us a complete visual rendering (fig. 8, on page 62), as well as an alphabet in which the letters are formed by the fingers of the human hand (fig. 9, page 63). These systems certainly possess a much longer history, but it is the coinciding at the end of the sixteenth century and the beginning of the seventeenth of these additions foreign to the ancient theory of

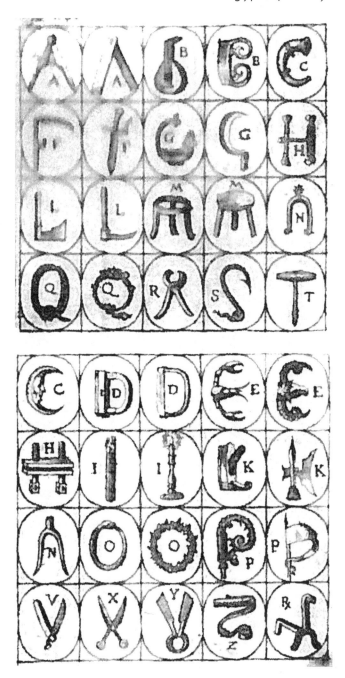

Figure 7. Cosma Rosselio,
Thesaurus artificiosae memoriae, 1579.

Figure 8. Giambattista della Porta,
Ars reminiscendi, 1602.

the *Ars memorativa* that I am hoping to identify. At first glance, these letters seem to be strictly obeying the precepts of the *imagines agentes*, to the extent that they assume ridiculous or obscene positions, but their role is no longer that of *personae* at all. In fact, there is no reason then to wonder about what they are doing or what they might mean, as all they give us to read is the shape of their contortions.

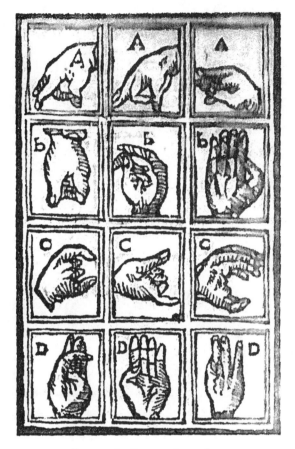

Figure 9. Cosma Rosselio,
Thesaurus artificiosae memoriae, 1579.

The object-letters or their animal avatars were therefore what organized these sites: it should be no cause for surprise that the human
body or hand were made into locational indicators, as they would also
be transformed into sites in turn several years later. But something was
happening then at the end of the sixteenth century, perhaps under the
influence of the hieroglyphic model that these curious alphabets irresist-
ibly brought to mind. The accent would be increasingly placed on the
use of these figurative alphabets to form *imagines*. At the same time, and
by that fact alone, the attention paid to the artificial memory of words
that left Cicero indifferent and that the Middle Ages seemed to hold in

no higher esteem is proclaimed. So where the ancients suggested simple stenographic signs for tool words such as conjunctions or prepositions,[34] at the end of the Renaissance, the imagination strives to represent *per* or *hoc*. In truth, Peter of Ravenna was already trying to do this but remained scrupulously faithful to the imagines agentes, placing Thomas before Eusebius to form *TE* and Eusebius before Thomas to form *ET*. By means of alphabets consisting of people, letters were simply personified, with the theatrical removing the hieroglyphic. But later authors all advised the blending of these alphabets. By juxtaposing or coordinating the figures of animals, objects, and human bodies, whole or in parts, they gave a strong impression of "playing at hieroglyphs." In this way it was suggested that *HOC* could be written in the following way: a body with arms and legs spread apart to depict the *H*, which was holding a circle in the right hand and half a gourd in the left hand.[35] In this instance, and *stricto sensu,* the (pseudo-) hieroglyphic image is clearly the equivalent of a word. The technique was becoming systematized at the beginning of the sixteenth century. At the same time the figurative portrayal of the letter, which could appear somewhat wasteful, was being abandoned, and bountiful tables of the equivalencies of tool words and syllables capable of visualization were being drawn up. The translation into images therefore no longer needed any symbolic mediation. Adam Bruxius established, in his *Simonides redivivus,*[36] a veritable annotated lexicon for numbers, words without figures, tool words, and abstract notions. The various alphabets were collated under the sole types of the word. No image would ever again catch the hieroglyphic dream in its snare: every letter was accompanied by an implacably verbal list of proper names, animal names, or the mention of the *res figurae similis* as *caput tauri* for *D*. As for the translation of abstract notions,

---

34. See *De oratore,* II, 359.
35. For more, see the work by Marafioti cited on page 56. It can be found again in the work of Adam Bruxius cited on this page, *Simonides redivivus siue ars memoriae et obliuionis . . . tabulis expressa* (Leipzig, 1610).
36. Adam Bruxius.

it reduced the metaphorical, mnemonic, or simply phonetic processes in which the few remaining traces of the "hieroglyphic" language of a bygone age had been enlisted to one same principal of lexical synonymy. In this way, *constans* could be transcribed by *hedera*, *albus* by *lilium*, and *nudus* by *nidus*. This was followed by a *Nomenclator mnemonicus* with a somewhat mysterious purpose that classed the *nomina*, then the *verba* in alphabetical order. This gave, ipso facto, a series of possible images for all syllables; for *ab: abies, abas,* and so on; for *ac: accipiter, acus,* and so forth.

Toward the Rebus

We are therefore not very far from the rebus at the point when the value of an image was determined by its sound (albeit partial and restricted to the initial one in the case of the alphabets) and not by what it represented. So the fact that rebuses began proliferating in the arts of memory and the well-known case of the figurative sonnet provided by Palatino in 1540 and reproduced in the *Ars reminiscendi* by della Porta for its exemplary value is far from being an isolated indication of the interpenetration of the two arts.[37] The play on words soon made its presence felt, but in the simple form of the approximation that made it possible to find a figuration for a word that otherwise would not have one.[38] This is how we can "translate *apud* by *caput.*" (This path had already been laid by the *Rhetorica ad Herennium.*[39]) The process was refined and codified at a later date. Rhetoric brings the backing of its metalanguage, and this ensured that an individual could very seriously, thanks to prothesis, transform *per* into *aper* (wild boar), thanks to epenthesis make *la pena una penna,* and thanks to

---

37. The very most that can be said is that it is the sole example we have in our *artes memoriae* of an illustrated rebus. It has often been reproduced, most recently in the book by Jean Ceard and Jean-Claude Margolin, *Le Rébus à la Renaissance* (Paris: Maisonneuve et Larose, 1987).
38. They cannot be found, however, despite Volkmann's claim, in the *Ars memorativa* by Guillaume Lelièvre, published in Paris in 1520.
39. See above, footnote 12.

aphesis extract *ove* from *dove* or *menta* from *elementa*. I have borrowed these examples from Gesualdo, but everyone will recognize them as classical examples of the type.

The transformations that took place in the arts of memory over the course of the years unfailingly followed in this direction. I need only cite as proof the examples added by Le Cuirot to his translation of *Gazophylacium* by Lambert Schenkel. These could only be the work of his pen, as they play on French linguistic structures. For example, for memorizing the strange name of a philosopher mentioned by Cicero, Alabandensis, for which Schenkel suggests the series of a wing, a band, and a sword, Le Cuirot proposes a band or a troop of children divided into six rows.[40] An even more characteristic example perhaps would be this one from the *Dialogue* in which, in order to remember the name of the emperor Oto, one would picture an Ottoman bearing a sack on his back, not for phonetic emphasis, but I think so that "one removes the back from the Ottoman" in order to get *Oto*. The innovation here resides in the henceforth strict application of the rebus principle.[41] It is so rigorously applied it gives the impression that the purpose has been shifted and that the ends have been made subordinate to the means. This is because it is hard to see how the technique of the rebus could be put into general use. The arbitrary nature of its fragmentation specifically makes it hard to memorize, and people can only remember a rebus thanks to its translation, since it can only be read once it has been translated.[42] Of dubious effectiveness on the mnemonic level, the examples of partial rebuses that flourished in the arts of memory reveal just how the game was being played. And didn't they, too, contribute to breaking the imago that had reigned since antiquity over the field of memory by stripping it of its proper meaning and replacing it with the rule of the letter and its dizzying

40. See *Gazophylacium*, 62.
41. For more on the rebus, see Eva Marie Schenck, *Das Bilderrätsel* (Hildesheim and New York: Georg Olms Verlag, 1973).
42. For a different opinion on the value of the rebus as a mnemonic technique, see Ceard and Margolin, *Le Rébus à la Renaissance,* 54ff.

combinations? The last symptom I have identified will complete this provisional demonstration.

The Direct Inscription

It was inevitable that things reached this point. The "innovators" Gesualdo and Marafioti, who had already succeeded in draining the *imago agens* by making it play the role of a connector, drew the logical conclusion that it was now necessary to move on to a more direct transcription. Both of them retained the ancient system next to their new art, but it seems to me that the parallels they established between the two only better emphasized the relay that was at work there. Following a text he cited on the hieroglyphs, Gesualdo went on to say: *"cosi noi collocamo nelli luoghi in due modi, primo immediatamente le parole sole senza immagine, secondo mediatamente le parole per via d'immagini. . . . Il primo modo conviene alli luoghi formati nelli numeri e nelle persone. Il secondo conviene alli luoghi stabili"* forms according to the traditional rules. Marafioti opposed the classical system in which a lamb opening its mouth was used for *Balatus* with his own system in which a *B* with wings was placed over the hand.[43] The rebus (and I do not view this as an accident) was therefore reduced to a letter. *The Storehouse of the Sciences,* which inscribes the hand as a secondary site on the walls of the primary site, brings to mind the reservations expressed by Johann-Heindrich Alsted, who was skeptical of the possibilities of placing the *imagines* on the hand and who favored a system of tablets of inscription.[44] I will bring this section to a close with an example that I believe will allow us to assess the extent and the radical nature of the reversal. Peter of Ravenna, who strove, as mentioned earlier, to apply the principle of *imagines agentes* to the memorizing of words, proposed remembering the syllable *BRA* by

---

43. Work cited above, footnote 29.
44. The book by J. H. Alsted, *Systema mnemoricum duplex . . . in quo artis memorativae praecepota* was published in Frankfurt in 1610, the same year as Lambert Schenkel's *Gazophylacium.*

imagining the phrase *Benedictum cum ranis seu rapis*. At the other end of the spectrum, *The Storehouse of the Sciences* diametrically opposed this with its belief that the syllable could replace the phrase. *BRA* would therefore mean "that Benedict traveling across a field stayed there to gather some turnips"[45] and to remember *BRA,* one could, if one liked, "picture" the syllable by replacing it with a bracelet.

The mnemonic writing technique had therefore become encrypted, like those secret scripts that della Porta and Blaise de Vigenère used (at almost the same time) to disclose mysteries and tricks. In this way the materialization of the letter or the syllable collided with the removal of the hieroglyphic concept's sacred character. It was now well known that one could write with images without rattling an infinite number of divine connotations. It was equally known that the secret (necessarily well protected) of these individual figures, to which all artificial techniques of memorization necessarily resort, does not have, a priori, anything at all in common with the sacred. The very triviality of certain complex groupings proves better than anything that henceforward the image no longer had any privileged connection with some higher content. Having reached this point, the *Ars memorativa* came face-to-face with the contemporary blossoming of the art of encryption, which was more clearly codified and perhaps of a usefulness that was less questionable. Most importantly, it found itself ensnared in the insurmountable contradiction that this kinship itself revealed. By drawing away from the theatrical path, by giving a cold shoulder to symbolic figures and turning toward play with letters, the artificial memory was surely responding to the commands of the master encoders of the new times who prescribed a series of transpositions, the better to scramble the code, but it attracted its decoder, natural memory, into a game that would prove fatal to both of them. This ensured that its only recourse, in this respect, was to vanish.

I cannot help but be pleased by this suicide of the *Ars memoria*

---

45. *Storehouse of the Sciences*, 235.

because it offers valuable confirmation of the conclusions I drew, some eight years ago, on the development of the emblematic image during that same era.[46] We can clearly see how interest shifted from the figure to the letter and from the symbol to the word. It was this that was now offered, under a variety of avatars, to curiosity; it was upon this that the ultimate fires of the hieroglyphic mystery were concentrated because very little remained of what had been the practice of mnemonic techniques during the heyday of Neoplatonism in the fifteenth century. Caught in the web of the discourse to be memorized, the hieroglyph once again became what it never truly ceased to be: one scriptural sign among others, albeit one somewhat less popular than the others. Everything fell out as if this new horizontal subordination had undone the ancient vertical relationship to Divine Wisdom. Regimented within the Memoria, the fourth part of Rhetoric, it now spoke clearly and—the ultimate irony—more clearly than the syllables and letters that, during the seventeenth century, irrevocably wrested from it the gift of secrecy.

---

46. "Le statut de l'image dans les livres emblématiques en France de 1580 à 1630," in *L'Automne de la Renaissance 1580–1630*, ed. J. Lafond and A. Stegmann (Paris: Vrin, 1981), 163–78.

The Ancient Sources of Initiatic Transmission in Freemasonry

The Royal Art and the Classical Art of Memory

By Charles B. Jameux

The study of the Torah is greater than the rebuilding of the Temple

TALMUD, MEGILLA TREATISE, 166

IT IS OFTEN SAID THAT EVERY Freemason, at least once in his lifetime as an initiate, goes through a phase of self-doubt about his membership in the Masonic Order and his reasons for staying with it.

This article originally appeared in the magazine *Points de Vue Initiatiques* (Initiatory Perspectives), issue no. 100 (special issue devoted to the sources and origins of speculative Freemasonry), in December 1995. It was later published under the title, "Les sources antiques de la transmission initiatique en franc-maçonnerie: art classique de la mémoire," in *La franc-maçonnerie—histoire et dictionnaire,* ed. Jean-Luc Maxence (Paris: Robert Laffont, 2013) and appears here by permission. Thank you to Noel Castelino for the English translation.

"What am I doing here? What is the point of it all?" he asks himself, wondering whether or not he should continue as a Freemason. This period of self-questioning may be likened to a mood, and it is fairly well known to be short-lived.

By contrast, I have always felt that for the rest of the time (and this fact is less often noted), Freemasons are not given to asking questions about the origins of their practices and, ultimately, about the deeper meaning of Freemasonry and the experiences that they live within it. They remind me of churchgoers who may know what is going on in the liturgy and have some vague notion of its meaning but no longer possess any idea of why there is a service, why one goes to church, what exactly happens there, and so on.

In other words, I have observed that the members of regular and traditional Freemasonry generally know the "meaning" of the symbols but are not aware of their whys and wherefores. Similarly, they have some broad knowledge of the ritual but cannot explain why rituals exist. They can often define *initiation* but are incapable of saying how it works. They cannot pinpoint the psychological mechanisms by which a process, generally regarded as being proper to the individual, can be transmitted at a psychological level from one individual to another and, at what might be called the level of the group, from the lodge to the individual.

As to myself, I am of course well aware that I belong to this category of Freemasons. For it must be said that the historical origins of speculative Masonry (the birth of which, as is generally known, took place well before 1717 in the British Isles, and more specifically in Scotland and England) are as yet obscure. Moreover, and although I have been seeking answers to these questions for well-nigh twenty years, I have been unable to find any satisfactory ones, which is perhaps quite understandable, given the complexity and range of the problems involved.

These personal admissions aside, the problems are truly complex and, above all, basic. They involve a great deal more than my own Masonic research. At the same time, they bind us to a common and identical task of reflecting on our speculative origins. I might summarize this task of reflection in a few questions that I have always been confronted with.

What is the nature of the initiation that is proposed and developed by speculative Freemasonry? What is it that is passed on? How is it passed on in this particular fashion; that is, by the use of metaphors taken from the world of the building and construction trades? In other words, has the nature of our initiatic approach come to us by direct descent from its supposedly recent historical origin, which is, broadly speaking, from the "craft" Freemasonry that immediately preceded it? Or rather has it been derived by spiritual influence from an ancient tradition belonging to a far earlier age?

How and why is it that, in this system of metaphors drawn from the world of the building and construction trades, the image of the temple was established from the very outset as the central image of nascent, speculative Freemasonry in its three main forms: Solomon's temple, the Universal temple, and the interior temple? How and why is it that the constant use of symbols and the effective practice of ritual have always been the established criteria of authentic Masonry?

And finally, there is the issue of the degrees. Why is it that no sooner had the first three symbolic degrees been set up and differentiated than a large number of additional ones were created in their wake? Our detractors speak of vanity and refer in a pejorative manner to a "multiplication" of degrees. I shall try to show that this is not at all the case. It is clear that all these questions form, together, an important issue.

Two recent books by non-Masonic British historians came to my attention just three years ago and have prompted further thinking on my part. Both have a standpoint on the historical origins of speculative Freemasonry. However, the honest and rigorous approach of these non-Masonic historians has prevented them from drawing every possible inference from their discoveries. Nor do they arrive at all the "masonological" conclusions dictated by these inferences. One of them limits herself to describing an essential but insufficiently appreciated element in Western civilization, namely "the art of memory." The other describes the relationship that existed between the art of memory and nascent, speculative Freemasonry in Scotland in the late sixteenth and early seventeenth centuries. However, neither one (nor, as we shall see, French researchers such as Alain Bernheim or Edouard Maisondieu) makes full use of his or her discoveries. They merely suggest that the art of memory might have influenced the formation of speculative Freemasonry.

The first work is by Frances Yates: *The Art of Memory* (London: Routledge and Kegan Paul, 1966; French translation, *L'Art de la mémoire* [Paris: Gallimard, 1975]).

The second work, which is more widely known, is David Stevenson's *The Origins of Freemasonry: Scotland's Century 1590–1710* (Cambridge: Cambridge University Press, 1988; French trans., *Les origines de la franc-maçonnerie—Le siècle ecossais 1590–1710* [Paris: Éditions Télètes, 1993]).

The first part of this paper shall therefore be devoted to a short description of the intention and main theme of each work and will seek to highlight its originality from the standpoint of the issues concerned here. An attempt shall then be made to explain and provide ontological justification for a hypothesis concerning the origins of speculative Freemasonry and to show why it is not wholly absurd to imagine that the art of memory (at least in its classical form in the Middle Ages and during the Renaissance) quite simply bequeathed its mode of operation to speculative Freemasonry, which was then in its formative stages.

In passing (and this will be the third part of the present development), an attempt shall be made, on the documentary and historical level, to argue for the likelihood of what can presently be, for lack of historical proof, only a research hypothesis.

For Frances Yates, writing in 1966, Masonic historians "have to leave as an unsolved question the problem of the origin of 'speculative' Masonry, with its symbolic use of columns, arches, and other architectural features, and of geometrical symbolism, as the framework within which it presents a moral teaching and a mystical outlook directed towards the divine architect of the universe. . . . I would think that the answer to this problem may be suggested by the history of the art of memory, that the Renaissance occult memory, as we have seen it in Camillo's Theatre and as it was fervently propagated by Giordano Bruno, may be the real source of a Hermetic and mystical movement which used, not the real architecture of 'operative' Masonry, but the imagery or 'speculative' architecture of the art of memory as the vehicle of its teachings."[1] At the time when it was put forward, this thesis was an innovative one.

However, it went relatively unnoticed, and above all, it was not exploited to the extent that I believe it should have been.

It was only in 1988 that David Stevenson added the following commentary on the above passage: "This is perhaps too sweeping; in the Middle Ages and the Renaissance, obsessed with symbolism and imagery, any craft was likely to develop symbolism as arising entirely from the Renaissance art of memory is unconvincing. But through the Second Schaw Statutes the art of memory can now be directly linked to the development of Freemasonry, and the occult overtones the art had acquired contributed to the development of Masonic secrecy and ritual."[2]

This quote clearly points to a major discovery by Stevenson concerning late sixteenth century Scotland, one that I shall come back to shortly. However, Stevenson also comments on the facts presented by Frances Yates and on her hypothesis, especially as put forward in her chapter 13 ("Last Works on Memory"), which is about Giordano Bruno. The following passage from Yates establishes the link between the two authors:

I have drawn attention in my other book to the rumour that Bruno was said to have founded a sect in Germany called the

---

1. Yates, *The Art of Memory*, 206, 304, all page numbers refer to the 1966 edition.
2. Stevenson, *The Origins of Freemasonry*, 96.

"Giordanisti," suggesting that this might have something to do with the Rosicrucians, the mysterious brotherhood of the Rosy Cross announced by manifestos in the early seventeenth century in Germany, about which so little is known that some scholars argue that it never existed. Whether or not there is any connection between the rumoured Rosicrucians and the origins of Freemasonry, first heard of as an institution in England in 1646 when Elias Ashmole was made a Mason, is again a mysterious and unsettled question. Bruno, at any rate, propagated his views in both England and Germany, so his movements might conceivably be a common source for both Rosicrucianism and Freemasonry. The origins of Freemasonry are wrapped in mystery, though supposed to derive from mediaeval guilds of "operative" Masons, or actual builders. No one has been able to explain how such "operative" guilds developed into "speculative" Masonry, the symbolic use of architectural imagery in Masonic ritual. . . .

I think that the answer to this problem may be suggested by the history of the art of memory, that the Renaissance occult memory may be the real source of a Hermetic and mystical movement which used, not the real architecture of "operative" Masonry, but the imagery or "speculative" architecture of the art of memory as the vehicle of its teachings. A careful examination of the symbolism, both of Rosicrucianism and of Freemasonry, might eventually confirm this hypothesis. Such an investigation does not belong within the scope of this article, though I will point to some indications of the lines on which it might be conducted.

The supposedly Rosicrucian manifesto or *Fama Fraternitatis* of 1614 speaks of mysterious *rotae* or wheels, and of a sacred "vault" the walls, ceiling and floor of which are divided into compartments each with their several figures or sentences. This could be something like an occult use of artificial memory. Since for Freemasonry there are no records until much later, the comparison here would be with Masonic symbolism of the late seventeenth and eighteenth centuries and particularly, perhaps, with the symbolism of that branch of Masonry known as the "Royal Arch." Some of the old prints, banners, and aprons of Royal Arch Masonry, with their designs of arches, columns, geometrical figures and emblems, look as though they might well be in the tradition of occult memory. That tradition would have been entirely forgotten, hence the gap in the early history of Masonry.

The advantage of this theory is that it provides a link between later manifestations of the Hermetic tradition in secret societies and the main Renaissance tradition. For we have seen that Bruno's secret had been a more or less open secret in the earlier Renaissance when Camillo's Theatre was such a widely publicised phenomenon. The secret was the combination of the Hermetic beliefs with the techniques of the art of memory. In the early sixteenth century this could be seen as belonging naturally into a Renaissance tradition, that of the "Neo-platonism" of Ficino and Pico as it spread from Florence to Venice. It was an example of the extraordinary impact of the Hermetic books on the Renaissance, turning men's minds towards the *fabrica mundi,* the divine architecture of the world, as an object of religious veneration and a source of religious experience. In the later sixteenth century, the more troubled age in which Bruno passed his life, the pressures of the times, both political and religious, may have been driving the "secret" more and more underground, but to see Bruno only the propagator of a secret society (which he may have been) would be to lose his full significance.

For this secret, the Hermetic secret, was a secret of the whole Renaissance. As he travels from country to country with his "Egyptian" message Bruno is transmitting the Renaissance in a very late but a peculiarly intense form. This man has to the full the Renaissance creative power. He creates inwardly the vast forms of his cosmic imagination, and when he externalises these forms in literary creation, works of genius spring to life, the dialogues which he wrote in England. Had he externalised in art the statues which he sculpts in memory, or the magnificent fresco of the images of the constellations which he paints in the *Spaccio della bestia trionfante,* a great artist would have appeared. But it was Bruno's mission to paint and sculpt within, to teach that the artist, the poet, and the philosopher are all one, for the Mother of the Muses is Memory. Nothing comes out but what has first been formed within, and it is therefore within that the significant work is done. . . .

For if Memory was the Mother of the Muses, she was also to be the Mother of Method. Ramism, Lullism, the art of memory—all those confused constructions compounded of all the memory methods which crowd the later sixteenth and early seventeenth centuries—are symptoms of a search for method. Seen in the context of this growing search, or urge, it is not so much the madness of Bruno's systems as their uncompromising determination to find a method which seems significant.

At the end of this attempt to make a systematic summary of Bruno's works on memory, I would emphasise that I do not claim to have fully understood them. When later investigators have discovered more about the almost unknown and unstudied subjects with which this book attempts to deal, the time will be ripe for reaching a fuller understanding of these extraordinary works, and of the psychology of occult memory, than I have been able to achieve. What I have tried to do, as a necessary preliminary for understanding, is to attempt to place them in some kind of a historical context. It was the mediaeval art of memory, with its religious and ethical associations, which Bruno transformed into these occult systems which seem to me as possibly having a triple historical relevance. They may be developing Renaissance occult memory in the direction of secret societies. They certainly still contain the full artistic and imaginative power of the Renaissance. They announce the part to be played by the art of memory and Lullism in the growth of the scientific method.

But no historical net, no examination of trends or influences, no psychological analysis, may ever quite serve to snare or to identify this extraordinary man, Giordano Bruno, "the Magus of Memory."[3]

For my part, I feel that the historical and ontological hypothesis put forward by Frances Yates is worthy of consideration and, therefore, that it should be considered and examined. To put it briefly, she establishes a historical link between the appearance of the speculative, Masonic approach and Giordano Bruno, his influence and his English and German travels, and above all the imaginary and speculative architecture of the classical art of memory, as a medium of the teaching that Bruno is supposed to have bequeathed to Scotland. "Nothing comes out but what has first been formed within, and it is therefore within that the significant work is done."[4] However, this viewpoint clearly lacked the underpinning of facts proper to Freemasonry that could form a Masonic missing link. This missing link, and a properly Masonic one at that, was discovered in 1988 when David Stevenson identified it in the second Schaw Statutes, the professional statutes of Scottish craft Masonry issued in Edinburgh in 1599.

Article 13 of these statutes, which were "operative" (but contain the seeds of the symbolic practices of speculative Masonry to come), states that it was the role of the warden of Kilwinning Lodge to test "euerie fallowe of craft and euerie prenteiss" in "the art of memorie and science thairoff."[5] In his preface to the French translation of Stevenson's work, the eminent French historian and specialist in Masonic studies, Alain Bernheim, provides an interesting description of the Scottish historian's ideas. In passing, it might be noted that it was an easy matter for Bernheim to make short shrift of Frances Yates's albeit astutely and intelligently presented assumption of a link between the existence of a spiritual and speculative architecture and "Royal Arch" Masonry. For Yates, after all, was not a Mason. The mistake in her assumption, which

---

3. Yates, *The Art of Memory*, 302–307.
4. Yates, *The Art of Memory*, 305.
5. Stevenson, *The Origins of Freemasonry*, 45.

was hers alone, cannot be laid against Stevenson. This point, as shall be seen, has been noted by Bernheim himself. Here, all the same, is Alain Bernheim's excellent analysis of Stevenson's work in his penetrating preface:[6]

> It is on page 17 of his introduction that Stevenson puts forward the central argument of *The Origins of Freemasonry,* which is that the Medieval contribution of craft organization and legend provided some of the ingredients essential to the formation of Freemasonry, but that the process by which these were combined with other ingredients did not occur until around 1600, and that it occurred in Scotland. Aspects of Renaissance thought were then spliced onto the Medieval legends, along with an institutional structure based on lodges and the rituals and the secret procedures for recognition known as the Mason Word. It is in this late Scottish Renaissance phase that, according to the main argument of this book, modern Freemasonry was born. To support this argument, Stevenson quotes seven words taken from the second Schaw Statutes of 1599, "the art of memorie and science thairoff" [Stevenson, *Les origines de la franc-maçonnerie,* 49]. He believes that these words illustrate those "aspects of Renaissance thought" referred to by him in the introduction to *The Origins of Freemasonry* and explains the matter thus: "Art of Memory was not merely a rather strange and clumsy term for what had been memorized as has been assumed in the past. It was a technique for memorizing things which had its roots in ancient Greece . . . becoming, in the Middle Ages and Renaissance something that was highly symbolic and even occult . . . the three simple words 'art of memory' may be taken as proof that from the first the Schaw lodges were at least dabbling in occult and mystical strands of late Renaissance thought." Stevenson acknowledges

---

6. Alain Bernheim's foreword to the French edition of Stevenson, *Les origines de la franc-maçonnerie,* v–vi, here translated into English.

however that "it is not easy to understand the meaning of the statutes if they are considered in isolation. The interpretation of them which follows is therefore partly inspired by additional information from other sources, especially early lodge minute books and the early Masonic catechisms [Stevenson, *Les origines de la franc-maçonnerie,* 36].

In order to interpret these three words of the Schaw statutes, the *art of memory,* as the vector of a hermetic connotation, Stevenson relies on Frances Yates. For, in her book *The Art of Memory,* after having referred to the unresolved problem of the origin of "speculative" Freemasonry with its symbolic use of columns and arches and of geometrical symbolism as a framework within which it presents a moral teaching and a mystical outlook directed toward the divine architect of the universe, Yates adds: "I would think that the answer to this problem may be suggested by the history of the art of memory . . . "[quoted in Stevenson, *Les origines de la franc-maçonnerie,* 96]. It hardly need be emphasized that the symbolic elements referred to by Yates were introduced into Freemasonry by Preston and Hutchinson in the second half of the eighteenth century and that there can be no way, barring solid proof, by which this introduction can be predated by two centuries. The use of this quotation from Yates is a revealing indication of Stevenson's tendency toward syncretism. He follows the quotation with the following observation: ". . . through the second Schaw statutes, the art of memory can now be directly linked to the development of Freemasonry, and the occult tones the art had acquired contributed to the development of Masonic secrecy and ritual."

On all these points, I must make it clear that I cannot share Bernheim's strictures against Stevenson's syncretism. Indeed and even if Stevenson, precisely because he is not a Freemason, does not appear to have exploited all the possibilities inherent in his hypothesis, Alain

Bernheim does not seem to have grasped the full thrust of Stevenson's argument, nor has he examined it with the impartial and dispassionate approach called for by such a subject. Thus, for example, the notion of a Scottish nurturing soil on which his argument is based has long been known to many Masons. This is borne out, for example, by the following quotation from Goblet d'Alviella:[7]

> Finally, the general regulations of Scottish Freemasonry, the Schaw Statutes issued in 1598-1599, have come down to us and were used by Brother Murray-Lyon to write a masterly history of Freemasonry in Scotland with reference to the Edinburgh Lodge. It appears from this work that Master and Fellow Craft were equivalent terms in Scotland. An Entered Apprentice could not become a Master unless he had shown proof of memory and talent. . . .

But it is time now to address the object of this first part and explain the specific nature of this sophisticated system of artificial memory that historians call the "art of memory," the source (to a great extent in my view) of speculative or modern Freemasonry. David Stevenson briefly summarizes the art of memory as follows:

> The art of memory was a technique for improving the capacity of one's memory which developed in ancient Greece but is mainly known through Roman writers. It was held to be of particular value to orators and lawyers in memorising long speeches, but was also seen as being of much wider application in the ages before printing, and indeed before widespread and cheap availability of a medium on which to write; a capacious and well-organised memory was regarded as central to education and culture. The Greek mnemonic

---

7. Goblet d'Alviella, *Des origines du grade de maître dans la franc-maçonnerie* [On the Origins of the Master's Degree in Freemasonry] (first published in 1906, republished by Éditions Tredaniel in 1983), 34.

technique was based on a building. The student of the art was instructed to study some large and complex building, memorising its rooms and layout, and particular features or places in it. In doing this he should establish a specific order in which he visited the individual rooms and places. When memorising a speech, he should then imagine himself to be walking through this building on his set route, and in each of the loci or places he had memorised he should establish imagines or images which were to be attached to each argument or point in his speech. The order in which the images were placed on the journey through the building should correspond to the order in which the points were to be made in the speech. These "images" established in the "places" should be connected in some way with points being memorised. The connection could be simple and direct (say a weapon to represent a murder or war) or indirect and convoluted, based on quirks of an individual's mind making connections between images and concepts which would not make sense to others. Very often the images were human figures, and it was thought that unusual and striking images— beautiful or grotesque, comic or obscene—were easier to remember than the commonplace.

When he came to give his speech, the orator would in his own mind walk through the building on his set route, and each image in its set location would remind him of the point he should come to next in his speech. While usually concerned with simply remembering the salient points to be made in the right order, there was also some discussion in the Roman sources of a far more intensive use of the art by the highly skilled, whereby virtually every word of a speech could be memorized. . . .

The often human images which revealed their significance through their actions, dress and possessions may also be seen as being related to the figures of gods and the personifications of abstract concepts (such as virtues identifiable by their attributes) which were popular in the ancient world. In the Roman empire, for example, these were developed on the coinage into an elaborate "form of symbolical references to almost every possible activity of the State" which was closely linked with popular belief through the tendency to regard the personifications as minor gods. Peace holding an olive branch, or Abundance holding ears of corn and a cornucopia could be called, in a very broad sense, memory images, and indeed many other kinds of symbolism can be seen in the same way, for symbols or images have always been widely used to remind the beholder of certain things. . . . Above all, the art of memory was based on mental images which had no physical existence. It was usually based on real buildings and the real places within them, but the images assigned to these places were mental ones, and when using the artificial memory the building was visited in the mind. Moreover, many of the images employed in the art of memory were the inventions of the individual user of the technique, and would make no sense to anyone else, whereas the whole point of the iconography of personifications and saints was that the images should be understood by all. . . .

In the ancient world the art of memory was classified as an aspect of Rhetoric, but Cicero—himself an advocate of the art—classified memory as one of the three parts of the virtue of Prudence (the others being intelligence and foresight). In the long term this had great significance for the art of memory, for the virtues defined by Cicero (Prudence, Justice, Fortitude and Temperance) became accepted in the Middle Ages as the four cardinal virtues. Thus in time the art of memory, identified with prudence, came to be regarded as an aspect of ethics. The work of St. Augustine added further significance to memory, for he regarded it as one of the three parts of the soul (the others being understanding and will), and taught that through exploring the memory men could find a memory-image of God embedded in their own souls. What had begun as a utilitarian technique for improving the memory had come to be seen as being of importance in religion not just as a valuable method of imprinting religious truths on the mind, but also as something that in itself had moral value and would lead to knowledge of God.

The art, many varieties of which developed, was not always fully understood and was sometimes viewed with suspicion. Moreover, though in the Middle Ages it had a central place in the schemas of knowledge, it was nonetheless a minor place, and information about its development is scarce. Then, in the fifteenth and sixteenth centuries the art became highly fashionable. Manuscript works describing and developing the art of memory in new ways proliferated, and were joined by printed treatises from 1482 onwards. These often included lists of images to be learned and pictures or diagrams of buildings with places in which images were to be put. The revival of the art of memory was in part an aspect of the general fascination with the legacy of the ancient world which typifies the Renaissance. But the art was usually interpreted through the work of Medieval writers, and this led many who despised the "barbarous" immediate past of the Middle Ages to reject it in spite of its respectable classical origins. Moreover, the spread of printing was, by the sixteenth century, reducing the need for elaborate memory techniques. But one of the strands of the Renaissance thought to make the art of memory its own. Through Renaissance Neoplatonism, with its Hermetic core, the art of memory was once more transformed, this time into a Hermetic or occult art, and in this form it continued to take a central place in a central European tradition.

The first person to bring this new type of memory system to prominence was Giulio Camillo, who died in 1544. His activities aroused intense interest, especially in France and Italy, for he constructed an elaborate wooden model "memory theatre," attributing remarkable powers to its workings, but refusing to reveal them to anyone but the king of France. Alas, the secrets were never revealed, but Frances Yates' reconstruction of the theatre reveals it as having been based on the classical theatre as described by the

Roman architect Vitruvius, though with the addition of biblical influences, as demonstrated by the inclusion of the seven pillars of Solomon's House of Wisdom ("Wisdom hath builded her house, she hath hewn out her seven pillars"–Proverbs, 9.1). From the classical art of memory Camillo took memory-places and constructed wooden images to put in them. But these images were regarded as talismans which could summon the magical powers of the sun and the planets in accordance with theories derived from Hermetic writings. The utilitarian art of memory has thus been transformed into an occult method whereby man could understand the universe and harness its powers, the leap from an earthly building to the heavens being facilitated by the act that, though since ancient times the art of memory had usually been based on buildings, a variant of the tradition had sought its memory-places in the signs of the zodiac and the stars.

The other famous sixteenth century exponent of the Hermetic version of the art of memory was Giordano Bruno (1548–1600). He joined the Dominican monastic Order, which had a long tradition of interest in the art of memory, and is said to have become highly qualified in the art at any early age. Of course his art of memory owed nothing to the example of Camillo, and differed from it considerably; the classical elements are less prominent, the occult and mystical are dominant. A number of his works were largely concerned with memory, and they show that he saw the art as a Hermetic secret of the distant past primarily significant through the magical powers it could be used to summon. As compared with Camillo, he was infinitely more daring in the use of notoriously magical images and signs in the occult memory, for his ambitions as a Hermetic magus who sought to call on the powers of the universe were much greater than those of his predecessor.

Bruno's first work on memory was explicitly Hermetic; it opens with a dialogue in which a treatise on the art of memory is presented by Hermes himself. The art is seen as a revelation of Egyptian knowledge, and the ultimate aim of the system was to help the mind of man to ascend to the understanding of the divine and achieve oneness with it. The art had become "a magico-religious technique, a way of becoming joined to the soul of the world as part of a Hermetic mystery cult."

Giordano Bruno visited Paris in 1581–1583, and his first two works on memory were published there in 1582. He then moved to England, where his third work was printed in 1583, and almost immediately a controversy erupted over his ideas. During this controversy his cause was championed in print by a Scot living in London. Alexander Dickson had been born in Perthshire in 1558 and had studied at the University of St. Andrew's. Early in 1584 he published a treatise based on Bruno's first work, outlining the classical art of memory but setting it in a Hermetic Egyptian context much more openly than Bruno had done. This was quickly followed by two denunciations of the treatise (on religious grounds) by a Cambridge scholar, a defence of his work by Dickson, written under an assumed name, and a final attack from Cambridge.[8]

These two hypotheses put forward by Yates and Stevenson are unusual when it is realized that they can serve as a single and homogeneous hypothesis. And since they are generally little known to French Masons and also since, or so it appears to me, historians have made little or no reference to them since 1988, I have thought it necessary to quote substantial passages.

These writers have led me to formulate a hypothesis, the terms and bases of which are drawn from these two works. This hypothesis is that there actually exists a very deep analogy of structure and mode of operation between the art of memory (in its classical form) and speculative Freemasonry.

---

8. Stevenson, *The Origins of Freemasonry,* 87–91.

In other words, in order to derive speculative Freemasonry by analogy from the ancestral art that preceded it, I would say that:

- The Masonic symbols are *imagines*, the images of the art of memory;
- The Masonic degrees are *loci*, the places of the art of memory; i.e., basically they are the rooms of the great edifice between which the subject making his way moves about and goes forward in the keen process of understanding the lesser and greater mysteries;
- The Masonic rite (namely the totality of the open teaching proposed by Freemasonry) is the grand edifice in its entirety. In other words, to continue with metaphors from the building trade, the Masonic rite is that great imaginary and speculative building or architecture of the mind within which the seeker moves as in a temple as huge as the universe and large enough to house and shelter the immensity of the Divine. At each step, the seeker memorizes his freely undertaken obligation to practice virtue, or, as the Latin has it, *ad colendam virtutem.*

And should this hypothesis prove to be historically convincing, I would say finally that the establishment of "the symbolic use of architectural images," as Yates writes in *The Art of Memory,* would fairly account for the phenomenon, a passage from purely mental realities (*imagines* or images or again memory/symbols) to their incarnation in the "method" constantly and untiringly sought by Giordano Bruno (but now discovered by the gentlemen Masons, adepts of the art of memory). This is the method that we know today, in which "ritual and instruction" are imparted by a question-and-answer process. It is also embodied in the lodge trestleboards that are unfolded at the opening of the lodge and then folded when it is closed. What is still to be done, of course, and this is what Frances Yates also suggests, is to examine Masonic symbolism in the light of the art of memory and determine, in specific terms, the extent to which the Hermetist followers of the aging art of imagines and loci, in searching for the method, paved the way for the speculative framers of the Royal Art of thought.

At this point it must nevertheless be said that it is probably not quite necessary to take sides in the contemporary debate among English Masonic historians. This point has to be made especially in regard to an article by Colin Dyer on the origins of speculative Masonry, the conclusions of which closely approach the views put forward earlier by Eric Ward. Dyer believes that the movement that gave rise to speculative Masonry was a deliberate creation, very probably of a secret nature, that was not necessarily related in any way to the notion of building or to the building industry. Indeed, David Stevenson's research appears to establish the strong and constant presence, from 1599 to 1696, of purely speculative elements right within the Scottish operative lodges. This is a very important point for, whether or not these speculative elements have a Hermetic origin and whether or not they are more or less related to the late expression of the Renaissance in Scotland, the fact is that everybody agrees today that the symbolic use of mental images arising out of the depiction of tools of the craft represents a mode, peculiar to speculative Masonry, of the individual, initiatic transmission of moral, metaphysical, and spiritual teachings, and of the duties that flow from there. Besides, this general agreement is particularly attested to in the article "History":

> It would nonetheless seem that the classical form of words in English Freemasonry, referred to above, i.e. "a particular system of moral teaching, veiled in allegory and illustrated by symbols" is a definition sufficient for our purpose, provided that the word "moral" is not given too narrow a meaning and provided that it is broadened to include intellectual and spiritual components (this observation also refers to present-day Freemasonry). We shall therefore apply the term "speculative" to a form of Masonry in which the technical elements of the Mason's craft (the tools, materials, disposition and organisation of the Lodge etc.) are cloaked in a symbolic meaning

that conveys a teaching in the different registers referred to above, and this rule shall be followed regardless of the composition of this Masonry, namely whether its members are operative, speculative or both.[9]

Such a traditional state of mind can therefore be found constantly in the declarations of principles of every regular Grand Lodge. Thus, for example, the Grande Loge de France, the world's first Masonic body to work in the Ancient and Accepted Scottish Rite, stated in article V of its declaration of principles on 5th December 1955:

> V. With respect to principles other than those defined above, the Grande Loge de France refers to the Old Charges, especially as regards compliance with the traditions of Freemasonry, and as regards the scrupulous and proper practice of the Ritual and Symbolism as the means of access to the initiatic content of the Order.

Let us now look at the symbols of speculative Masonry and examine their functions rather than their "meaning." Are they part of the art of memory? If so, what part? Conversely, does the art use symbols, and if so, to what end?

Looking at the question from the viewpoint of the symbols of speculative Masonry themselves, there is of course no need whatsoever for lengthy discourse. The symbols, especially those borrowed from the building craft, whether in the first, second, or third degrees, remind the Freemason of the goals and ideals to which he has subscribed and the moral qualities and forms of behavior whose practice and observance lead to the achievement of these ideals. But above all, they work on the initiate as if their fixed and permanent presence (in the temple

---

9. "History," in *Dictionnaire thématique illustré de la franc-maçonnerie* (edited by Lhomme, Maisondieu, and Tomaso), 251.

and in the texts) were intended to remind him of his duties: to shun vice and practice the virtues of brotherly love, relief, and truth; polish the rough ashlar, bring it into due form, and make it fit for use: subdue his passions and build a tomb for his vices.

But it might asked, by way of an objection, whether this memory function, one might say this "calling to attention" of the Mason, echoes or corresponds in any way to the classical and ancient art of memory, and whether its elements might allow for the inference today that there probably was a direct line of descent (or at the least a direct line of spiritual influence) linking the nascent Masonic symbols to their immediate predecessors, the imagines (images) or intentiones (intentions).

Frances Yates's work suggests that the answer may be affirmative. Indeed, this work highlights vital facts that point to the undeniable presence of the symbols (deriving from the "images") used as a means of remembering and relates them to the images the value of which medieval scholasticism sought to foster and enhance (through the efforts of Saint Thomas Aquinas and Albertus Magnus, working on the basis of a rediscovered Aristotle). A quote from Thomas Aquinas on his four personal precepts on art might be apt here:

Tullius (and another authority) says in his Rhetoric that memory is not only perfected from nature but also has much of art and industry: and there are four (points) through which a man may profit for remembering well.

(1) The first of these is that he should assume some convenient similitudes of the things which he wishes to remember; these should not be too familiar, because we wonder more at unfamiliar things and the soul is more strongly and vehemently held by them; whence it is that we remember better things seen in childhood. It is necessary in this way to invent similitudes and images because simple and spiritual intentions slip easily from the soul unless they are as it were linked to some corporeal similitudes, because human cognition is

stronger in regard to the sensibilia. Whence the memorative (power) is placed in the sensitive (part) of the soul.

(2) Secondly, it is necessary that a man should place in a considered order those (things) which he wishes to remember, so that from one remembered (point) progress can easily be made to the next. Whence the Philosopher says in the book *De memoria*: "some men can be seen to remember from places. The cause of which is that they pass rapidly from one (step) to the next."

(3) Thirdly, it is necessary that a man should dwell with solicitude on, and cleave with affection to, the things which he wishes to remember; because what is strongly impressed on the soul slips less easily away from it. Whence Tullius says, in his Rhetoric, that "solicitude conserves complete figures of the simulacra."

(4) Fourthly, it is necessary that we should meditate frequently on what we wish to remember. Whence the Philosopher says in the book *De memoria* that "meditation preserves memory" because, as he says "custom is like nature. Thence, those things which we often think about we easily remember, proceeding from one to another as though in a natural order."[10]

Yates has her own comments to make on this recourse to images (that is, basically, symbols that, from the very origins of speculative Masonry, were a determining criterion of regularity). And since the period in question precedes the seventeenth century, her comments prefigure the psychological mainsprings at work in the process of initiatic transmission in Freemasonry.

It has sometimes been a matter for surprised comment that the age of scholasticism, with its insistence on the abstract, its low grading of poetry and metaphor, should also be an age that saw an extraordinary efflorescence of imagery, and of new imagery, in religious art. Searching for an explanation of this apparent anomaly in the words of

---

10. Quoted in Yates, *The Art of Memory*, 74–75.

Thomas Aquinas, the passage in which he justifies the use of metaphor and imagery in the Scriptures has been quoted. Aquinas has been asking the question of why the Scriptures were imagery since "to proceed by various similitudes and representations belongs to poetry which is the lowest of all of the doctrines." He is thinking of the inclusion of poetry with Grammar, the lowest of the liberal arts, and enquiring why the Scriptures use this low branch of knowledge. The reply is that the Scriptures speak of spiritual things under the guise of corporeal things "because it is natural to man to reach the intelligibilia through the sensibilia because all our knowledge has its beginning in sense." This is a similar argument to the one that justifies the use of images in the artificial memory. It is extremely curious that those in search of scholastic justification for the use of imagery in religious art should have missed the elaborate analyses of why we may use images in memory given by Albertus and Thomas.[11]

However, this art of memory, in its classical form in the medieval period, was not merely a technique of memorizing, a method of artificial memory, a mnemotechnic device. Fostered by the Dominicans, of whom more shall be said below, the art established image-symbols and mnemotechnic signs, conceived before their time, to give men the desire to "shun vice and practise [Masonic] virtue." As Yates puts it:

> It is extremely probable that Albertus Magnus would have known of the *mystical rhetorics* of the Bolognese school, for one of the most important of the centres established by Dominic for the training of his learned friars was at Bologna. After becoming a member of the Dominican Order in 1223, Albertus studied at the Dominican house in Bologna. It is unlikely that here should have been no contact between the Dominicans at Bologna and the Bolognese school of *dictamen*. Boncompagno certainly appreciated the friars, for in his *Candelabrium eloquentiae* he praises the Dominican and Franciscan

---

11. Yates, *The Art of Memory*, 78–79.

preachers. The memory section of Boncompagno's rhetoric therefore perhaps foreshadows the tremendous extension of memory training as a virtuous activity which Albertus and Thomas (who was of course trained by Albertus) recommend in their *Summae*. Albertus and Thomas, it may be suggested, would have taken for granted—as something taken for granted in an earlier mediaeval tradition—that "artificial memory" is concerned with remembering Paradise and Hell and with virtues and vices as "memorial notes."

Moreover we shall find that in later memory treatises which are certainly in the tradition stemming from the scholastic emphasis on artificial memory, Paradise and Hell are treated as "memory places," in some cases with diagrams of those "places" to be used in "artificial memory." Boncompagno also foreshadows other characteristics of the later memory tradition, as will appear later.

We should therefore be on our guard against the assumption that when Albertus and Thomas so strongly advocate the exercise of "artificial memory" as a part of Prudence, they are necessarily talking about what we should call "mnemotechnics." They may mean, amongst other things, the imprinting on memory of images of virtues and vices, made vivid and striking in accordance with the classical rules, as "memorial notes" to aid us in reaching Heaven and avoiding Hell.

The scholastics were probably giving prominence to, or reviewing and re-examining, already existing assumptions about "artificial memory" as an aspect of their review of the whole scheme of the virtues and vices. This general revision was made necessary by the re-discovery of Aristotle, whose new contributions to the sum of knowledge, which had to be absorbed into the Catholic framework, were as important in the field of ethics as in other fields. The Nicomachean Ethics complicated the virtues, vices and their elements, and the new evaluation of Prudence by Albertus and Thomas is part of their general effort to bring virtues and vices up to date.

What was also strikingly new was their examination of the precepts of the artificial memory in terms of the psychology of Aristotle's *De memoria et reminiscentia*. Their triumphant conclusion that Aristotle confirmed the rules of Tullius put the artificial memory on an altogether new footing. Rhetoric is in general graded rather low in the scholastic outlook which turns its back on twelfth-century humanism. But that part of rhetoric which is the artificial memory leaves its niche in the scheme of the liberal arts to become, not only a part of a cardinal virtue but a worthwhile object of dialectical analysis.[12]

Here is Frances Yates on the rules put forward, before 1323, by the Dominican Bartolomeo da San Concordio:

(On order)

Aristotle in libro memoria: "Those things are better remembered which have order in themselves." Upon which Thomas comments: "Those things are more easily remembered which are well ordered, and those which are badly ordered we do not easily remember. Therefore those things which a man wishes to retain, let him study to set them in order."

Thomas in Seconda della seconda: "It is necessary that those things which a man wishes to retain in memory he should consider how to set out in order, so that from the memory of one thing he comes to another."

(On similitudes)

Thomas in Seconda della seconda: "Of those things which a man wishes to remember, he should take convenient similitudes, not too common ones, for we wonder more at uncommon things and by them the mind is more strongly moved."

---

12. Yates, *The Art of Memory*, 60–61.

Thomas in Quivi medesimo (i.e., loc. cit.): "The finding out of images is useful and necessary for memory; for pure and spiritual intentions slip out of memory unless they are as it were linked to corporeal similitudes."

Tullio in Terzo della nuova Rettorica: "Of those things which we wish to remember, we should place in certain places images and similitudes." And Tullius adds that "the places are like tablets, or paper, and the images like letters, and placing the images is like writing, and speaking is like Reading."[13]

Yates here immediately raises a question that is, at the same time, an observation couched in the form of a personal commentary on the text. She tries to describe the psychological reaction of the practitioner of this form of art to the spiritual intentions put in words that could have come straight out of a Masonic instruction.

What are we, as devout readers of Bartolomeo's ethical work, intended to do? It has been arranged in order with divisions and sub-divisions after the scholastic manner. Ought we not to act prudently by memorising in their order through the artificial memory the "things" with which it deals, the spiritual intentions of seeking virtues and avoiding vices which it arouses? Should we not exercise our imaginations by forming corporeal similitudes of, for example, Justice and its sub-divisions, or of Prudence and its parts? And also of the "things" to be avoided, such as Injustice, Inconstancy, and the other vices examined?[14]

However, this is not the most astonishing aspect of the work. Frances Yates devotes a major, well-documented part of it to the intellectual and spiritual origins of this classical conception of the art of memory. In particular, she establishes the fact that most of the great

13. Yates, *The Art of Memory*, 87.
14. Yates, *The Art of Memory*, 88.

thinkers who championed the art were Dominicans who had founded a world-renowned school.

She mentions Thomas Aquinas, of course, as well as Albertus Magnus, Peter of Ravenna, Johannes Romberch, Cosmas Rossellius. And of course, she also refers to Jacobus Publicius, whose work on memory, the *Oratoriae artis epitome* (1482), printed in Venice, was the first treatise on this subject. An interesting sidelight here is the fact that the handwritten copy of a work by Publicius, *Ars oratoria,* lies in the British Museum, the copy having been made in 1460 by Thomas Swatwell, who was probably a monk in Durham.

Naturally, it is for others to argue (and perhaps reach conclusions) about whether the Dominican friars, as a preaching order in the late Middle Ages, ultimately made a contribution, around 1640–1696, to the foundation by "gentlemen masons" of an initiatic practice. I refer here to an initiatic practice based on the analogical use of symbols related chiefly to the building craft; that is, the initiatic practice that we continue to call "speculative Freemasonry."

However, I would say that if this were to be the case, then the impulse that led to the creation of speculative Freemasonry was threefold. There was first the Dominican conception of the art of memory; second the arrival in London, between 1583 and 1586, of the prestigious Dominican, Giordano Bruno; and third the contemporary teaching of this art at the Scottish Court. The last-named fact is attested to, in different ways, by the presence of Robert Schaw, Alexander Dickson, and William Fowler at the court of King James VI and his queen.

To conclude these remarks on the birth of Masonic symbolism, I would finally add that we perhaps have proof today of the importance of the art of memory in this event. This proof lies in the important and quite special place occupied by the liberal arts in several degrees of Freemasonry (especially in the Ancient and Accepted Scottish rite), for we know that one of the seven arts is rhetoric, and we also know that one of the parts of rhetoric, according to Cicero, is memory.

Invention is the excogitation of true things (*res*), or things similar to truth to render one's cause plausible; disposition is the arrangement in order of the things thus discovered; elocution is the accomodation of suitable words to the invented (things); memory is the firm perspective of the soul of things and words; pronunciation is the moderating of the voice and body to suit the dignity of the things and words.[15]

To introduce the next part of my paper in which (and here it is speculative Freemasonry that is concerned) I shall examine what is perhaps the most important part of the hypothesis that I am now developing, namely ideas of the lodge and the temple, it would not be out of place to look at the rules that were formulated (between 1298 and 1314) by the Dominican Giovanni di San Gimignano, in an enormously popular work for users of the art of memory:

- There are four things which help a man to remember well.
- The first is that he should dispose those things which he wishes to remember in a certain order.
- The second is that he should adhere to them with affection.
- The third is that he should reduce them to unusual similitudes.
- The fourth is that he should repeat them with frequent meditation.[16]

Let us imagine that this advice were to be transposed into a purely "speculative" framework and applied to men whose chosen goal was to transmit knowledge in an initiatic manner (in other words, an esoteric manner) and follow ethical and spiritual rules in the conduct of their lives and actions. Without question, they would be faced with a problem of method.

---

15. De Inventione, I, VII, 9, quoted in Yates, *The Art of Memory*, 8–9.
16. *Summa de exemplis*, VI, 42, quoted in Yates, *The Art of Memory*, 85–86.

They would have a choice of several possible approaches. For example, they might choose to use symbols or allegories to represent moral values. Then, the simple evocation of these symbols, made conventionally without any excessive recourse to conceptual language, would remind them of the primary goals, the commitments made in regard to the practice and observance of these values. In their choice of a homogeneous register of allegory and symbol, they would also have to take into account the precepts of the ancient art of memory. They would need to choose corporal symbols and materials that were obscure and striking enough to hold the attention of trusted adherents, and yet consistent enough with the goal in view so that their application would not discourage the candidate from any possibility of spiritual advancement and constructive progress. Finally, to perfect their method, these men would have to find a place in which to work together and think in a discreet atmosphere of peace, silence and recollection. They would decorate this place (this "locus") with carefully chosen symbols, give it an orientation and finally order it so as to relate it with its human purpose and facilitate its study. Finally, they would periodically and regularly meet in this place and, in an atmosphere of order and mutual benevolence, they would concelebrate the reasons for showing to the outside world a model of sociability based on love of one's neighbor, harmony, and justice.

I believe that this method, if applied, could lead these men to the creation of *speculative* Freemasonry by borrowing the vectors of the symbolism proper to the practitioners of craft Masonry and making use of these vectors.

My hypothesis here is that the earliest speculative Masons acted in this way to found our Initiatic Order that, to quote Frances Yates, they set up at the very outset in the form of "vast interior cathedrals of memory." Otherwise, I cannot very well see how to explain the fact that the temple has been a founding and central figure of speculative Freemasonry since its very origins. In particular, and to put it very clearly, the presence of Solomon's Temple in operative Masonry and in the craft tradition cannot by itself explain the extraordinary role of the temple as a multiform and protean figure in speculative Masonry, for, in its diverse forms, Solomon's Temple is used as a moral and physical framework for the degrees. It reminds us of the Temple of the Universe. We speak of "building our interior temple," with a semantic transfer of the word "temple" to the structure that houses the lodge and finally to the lodge itself, and so on.

At the same time, it must be said that this hypothesis (apart from the arguments that have been put forward) is not entirely a novel one, since David Stevenson laid, to a great extent, the foundations for it as early as 1988:

> The features of the classical art of memory which made it seem particularly relevant to the Mason craft are obvious. The art was based on moving through an elaborate building, and it was an art which was believed to give great powers to the adept by vastly increasing the capacity of the human memory. Thus this powerful art which, like other arts, believed it could enhance human capabilities and easily take on occult overtones, was in a sense based on the skills of the architect/mason. Frances Yates, though not aware of the reference in the Second Schaw Statutes to the art of memory, suggested a connection between the art, which used an architectural framework in the search for wisdom, and Freemasonry.
>
> What did Schaw and the Masons use the art of memory for? The general striving for mystical enlightenment is doubtless present, but, as has already been suggested, it was probably also employed for more mundane purposes such as memorising the Old Charges. The two are not entirely separable, however: the search for knowledge of the divide was based on Hermetic theories of ancient Egyptian knowledge, and Hermes and Egypt have an important place in the Old Charges. Finally, and most excitingly of all for an understanding of the emergence of Freemasonry, it will be argued in the next chapter that the seventeenth-century Masonic lodge may have been,

in one sense, a memory temple, an imaginary building with places and images placed in it as aids to memorising the secrets of the Mason Word and the rituals of initiation. William Schaw's injunction that Masons must be tested in the art of memory and the science thereof has been read by generations of Masonic historians but the significance of it has never been noticed. Yet that single short phrase provides a key to understanding major aspects of the origins of Freemasonry, linking the operative Mason craft with the mighty strivings of the Hermetic magus.[17]

It was stated at the beginning of this paper that there are grounds for extending the analogic hypothesis developed herein to the Masonic degrees, and for examining the extent to which they may be considered to have originated from the "places" (the Latin loci) of the ancient art of memory.

I believe that this question is a very complex one. Indeed, some people will probably find it simplistic to assume that nascent, symbolic Masonry, in the manner of the classic art of memory that located each thing and each image in a particular place in the great edifice, was able to allocate its symbols in groups and formalize the separation between groups through the construction and establishment of the degrees. A man of Goblet d'Alviella's stature, seeking the origins of the master's degree, referred to this kind of difficulty:

> Doubts may be raised over the existence of the Rosicrucians in the 16th and 17th centuries as a closed society using quasi-Masonic forms and professing a secret philosophy cloaked in symbols whose knowledge was reserved for adepts. But what cannot be contested is the existence, in the Middle Ages and during the Renaissance, of hermetic and "cabalistic" groups that transmitted doctrines, symbols and practices dating back to the first centuries of the Christian era,

---

17. Stevenson, *The Origins of Freemasonry*, 95–96.

in a language that was intelligible to their initiates alone. It is no less an established fact that, at a given time, these groups entered Freemasonry with everything they possessed. What really has to be ascertained is whether their action was limited to the introduction of those higher degrees which bear the mark of a hermetic origin, or whether they had already had an effect on the development of speculative Freemasonry.[18]

It may be observed, however, that such an analogy is not wholly devoid of interest, if we look at the way in which events transpired (on the Master's degree, in addition to Goblet d'Alviella, cf. Jean Rigaud's very relevant work) and to the constituted and established degrees.

It is known that it was a long time before the first three degrees, known as the symbolic degrees, took the form in which they are known today. It is also known that in the period described in Stevenson's book, Master and Fellow craft were still one and the same (there was as yet no corresponding degree for the Master). However, it can be seen that when the degrees were differentiated, they were allocated symbols (especially related to the building trade) that were specific to the degree. It can also be seen that even if the Master's degree was the only one to be given a legend and even if, as is the case in the English rites, all the operative symbols can be found in the three degrees, it is only in the degree for which it is specifically designed that a symbol has its meaning explained, revealed, and commented upon.

This mode of structuring of each symbolic degree cannot be explained solely by the fact that the founders of our speculative Order sought to put up obstacles against warped "disclosures" by society and, and the same time, preserve and transmit secrets, particularly by tightly sealing and partitioning the degrees from one another.

On the contrary, I believe that the deeper explanation of this fact

---

18. Goblet d'Alviella, *Des origines du grade de maître dans la franc-maçonnerie,* cf. p. 86 of the 1983 reprint.

is still visible today to every Freemason. In the continental brand of Freemasonry, this explanation is constituted by the lodge trestleboard in which all the symbols proper to the degree are traced, summarized, and memorized. In English rite workings, it is the tracing board on which the teachings are painted (very beautifully, as it happens). These teachings the Candidate for advancement must render to his brethren by rote and in their entirety. The fact is that even today we are not very far removed from the art of memory of our origins. This is why I believe that the most important act in a lodge (and the most important act in its ritual) occurs at the opening when the tracing board or floor-cloth is unfolded, and at closing when it is rolled up again. Between these two gestures, each and every Freemason obtains confirmation of the initiatic and psychological genuineness of his long-standing commit-ments. Between these two gestures, he recollects the close, "ontological" correspondence, which is also a moving correspondence, between the two structures to which he has eternally submitted his will; namely, the structure of his interior temple, which is also that of his wisdom and his joy, and the structure formed by the "vast cathedrals of memory" of the Masonic Order.

Another element of our symbolism (naturally, I do not consider this brief list to be an exhaustive one) points even today to the mnemonic and mnemotechnic character of our speculative origins. In 1875, at the Lausanne Convent of the Ancient and Accepted Scottish Rite, Freemasons drafting the instruction for one of the first three degrees suggested the following approach to the tracing board:

Question: What does the tracing board represent?

Answer: It is the emblem of memory, that precious faculty which is given to us to form our judgement in preserving the trace of all our perceptions.

For a full and methodical development of my ideas, I must still ask one question. Is it true that this broadly sketched hypothesis, in its essence, substantially answers the major questions raised at the outset? Does it also account for the existence and mode of operation of these Masonic degrees that are placed after the Master's degree, mainly, of course, in the Ancient and Accepted Scottish Rite?

I would say in this case that the resemblance with the classical art of memory is even more disturbing for the first three degrees, even if the date of 1801, when this rite was established in degrees that are still known today, is far later than the period studied by Stevenson, for as Michaël L. Segall has first explained, these degrees were set up as the repositories and guardians of ancient initiatic and esoteric traditions. Without these degrees, these traditions would have been lost and would have vanished from the universal consciousness.

Each of these degrees is furthermore committed, in particular through the use of numerous facts inspired by the Bible, in the Volume of the universal and Sacred Law, to the preservation of moral laws and spiritual values (cf. Henry C. Clausen) and to reminding Freemasons of them.

To this end, each degree is constituted by commentary, exegesis, and the putting into practice of the ritual around a legend that is quite specific and proper to this degree. The evocation of this legend, in the manner of the *Urszene* or "primal scene" in psychoanalysis, acts on the plane of the initiate's moral approach in the same way as the imagines, intentiones, res, and verba of the art of memory practiced by the Dominicans and Giordano Bruno.

Each of the 30 degrees is thus designed to represent one of the loci of the edifice in which a part of the total teaching lies in a segmented and separate manner. Albert Pike called it "morals and dogma"; that is, to put it exactly, ethics and knowledge. This was in 1871.

About fifteen years ago, I believe it was in 1980, I was party to a conversation in which the philosopher Henri Tort-Nouguès compared the A&ASR to a large mansion or, more precisely, to a castle. This castle, he said, had 33 rooms and each of them contained a treasure. In the manner of this philosopher and friend, I would say, for my part, that the Masonic initiation consists in going from one room to another and, at each step, "in remembering" as Gérard de Nerval put it in a famous letter.

This is my deep and intimate personal conviction today, after having long meditated on the discoveries made by Frances Yates and David Stevenson. Modern Freemasonry is a prestigious continuator of the ancient art of memory practiced around 1590 at the court of King James VI of Scotland, and it owes this status partly to Giordano Bruno's arrival in the British Isles in 1583.

And if, withal, this hypothesis should prove one day to be mistaken and be countered by new facts, there would still be something left to me, that something of which the Russian poet Shalamov spoke in regard to poetry after twenty years in the Kolyma prison: "In winter, it is my fortress."

Bibliography

Alciat, André. *Les emblèmes*. Reprint, Paris: Klincksiek, 1997.

Balavoine, Claudie. "Hiéroglyphes de la mémoire: Émergence et metamorphose d'une écriture hiéroglyphique dans les Arts de mémoire du XVIe and du XVIIe siècles." *XVIIe siècle,* no. 158 (January–March 1988): 51–68.

Bernheim, Alain. (cf. his entire work).

Camillo, Giulio. *Le théâtre de la mémoire*. Paris: Allia, 2007.

Carruthers, Mary. *Le livre de la mémoire*. Macula, 2002.

Désaguliers, René. *Les deux Grandes Colonnes de la franc-maçonnerie*. Paris: Éditions Dervy, 2012.

———. *Les Pierres de la franc-maçonnerie*. Paris: Éditions Dervy, 1995.

Garin, Eugenio. *Hermétisme et Renaissance*. Paris: Allia, 2001.

Gould, Robert Freke. *Histoire abrégé de la franc-maçonnerie*. Translated by Louis Lartigue. Paris: Edition Jean de Bonnot, 1997.

———. *A Concise History of Freemasonry,* London: Gale & Pole, 1904.

Horne, Alex. *Le Temple de Salomon dans la tradition maçonnique*. Monaco: Rocher, 1994.

Jameux, Charles B. "Les sources antiques de la transmission initiatique en franc-maçonnerie: L'art classique de la mémoire." In *La Franc-maçonnerie— Histoire et dictionnaire,* ed. Jean-Luc Maxence. Paris: Robert Laffont, 2013.

Langlet, Philippe. *Les textes fondateurs de la franc-maçonnerie*. Paris: Éditions Dervy, 2006.

Lantoine, Albert. *La franc-maçonnerie chez elle,* Geneva: Éditions Slatkine, 1981.

———. *La franc-maçonnerie écossaise en France*. Paris: Éditions Dervy, 2011.

L'Architecture et la franc-maçonnerie. Ordo Ab Chao, no. 62, 2011.

Lhomme, Jean, Édouard Maisondieu, and Jacob Tomaso, *Dictionnaire thématique illustré de la franc-maçonnerie.* Monaco: Rocher, 1993.

Mackey, Albert G. *An Encyclopedia of Freemasonry and Its Kindred Sciences.* Philadelphia: L. H. Everts & Co, 1884.

Maxence, Jean-Luc. *La franc-maçonnerie—histoire et dictionnaire* collection "Bouquins." Paris: Robert Laffont, 2013.

Paine, Thomas. *De l'origine de la franc-maçonnerie.* Paris: Prieuré, 1997; translation of *An Essay on the Origin of Freemasonry.* London: R. Carlile, 1818.

Rey, Olivier. *Itinéraire de l'égarement: Du role de la science dans l'absurdité contemporaine.* Paris: Le Seuil, 2003.

Russel, John. "Le tableau du loge du 1er degree." *Freemasonry Today*, no. 10 (Autumn 1999).

Spécificité du REAA. Ordo Ab Chao, nos. 48–49, 2003–4.

Stevenson, David. *Les origines de la franc-maçonnerie: Le siècle écossais 1570–1710.* Paris: Télétes, 1993; translation of *The Origins of Freemasonry: Scotland's Century, 1590–1710.* Cambridge: Cambridge University Press, 1988.

———. *Les premiers francs-maçons.* Ivoire-Clair, 2000; translation of *The First Freemasons: Scotland's Early Lodges and Their Members.* Aberdeen, Scotland: Aberdeen University Press, 1988.

Thomas, Jacques. *Tableaux de loge et gravures maçonniques.* Paris: Éditions Dervy, 2005.

Volkmann, Ludwig. *Ars memorativa.* Vienna, Austria: A. Schroll, 1929.

Ward, Eric. "The Birth of Freemasonry." *Ars Quatuor Coronatorum,* no. 91, 1978.

Yates, Frances A. *The Art of Memory.* London: Routledge and Kegan Paul, 1966.

———. *L'Art de la mémoire,* Paris: Gallimard (NRF), 1975; translation of *The Art of Memory.* Chicago: University of Chicago Press, 2001.

———. *Giordano Bruno et la tradition hermétique.* Paris: Éditions Dervy, 1996; translation of *Giordano Bruno and the Hermetic Tradition.* Chicago: University of Chicago Press, 1991.

Index